My Tara
A public art project by Michael Fortune

About this Project

My Tara is a project which set about documenting a range of people's experiences in relation to the Hill of Tara, County Meath. This publication is the culmination of a series of encounters I experienced in and around the hill during 2013. The material is diverse and includes photographs I have taken myself combined with emails, accounts and images I received from various people, young and old, over the course of the year.

I began this process of investigation in late 2012 with my first ground work taking place in early 2013. I took a series of approaches with regard to generating and collating the information included in this publication. The first, most visible method of gathering information took the form of a Facebook page and website which were advertised though flyers and posters that were distributed locally in businesses, the post office, shops, cafés etc. The website and Facebook page helped to highlight the project and move the investigation along, generating dialogue and public enquiry. Over the course of this period I designed and placed two large information boards on the Hill of Tara which outlined the project; replicating the online presence, but now in real life, present and physical on the hill.

It has been my experience on past projects that the methods of promotion and research mentioned above, while useful, cannot compare to 'on the ground' chats and encounters. Things move on and develop in a different way with this approach. Sometimes, you are simply provided with the information you require. Other times, by pure luck, chance or destiny you can unexpectedly end up having a quite intense, meaningful encounter with an individual and the material which they have about the place. This work has an unusual pace at times, results can come fast and slow, and it's often not until later when there is time to reflect that you realise what you have just experienced. Often, I'd have fixed ideas as to what I wanted but the scenario would change in front of my very eyes. Or I wouldn't see it until I'd be in the car going home or looking over photos later, on the computer. Sometimes, when I'd be aware of something shifting in front of my own eyes, like the time I spent with Richard Farrelly, I was bothered, excited and confused – such a big rush of new information.

Word of mouth in Ireland is an old-fashioned but trusted way of working. The mention of someone's name can mean a lot when approaching another, e.g. "I was talking to Tom Doyle the other day and he said you'd be a good person to talk to about the statue on the hill." Often the response to this is an Irish "not putting yourself out there" comment such as "Well, I don't know about that…" soon followed by a helpful "what do you want to know anyway?".

There is no science to this approach. In general, I feel Irish people still have an inbuilt nature of goodwill and hospitality, which is fantastic to experience when it's being played out in front of you. They will try to help you - even if it means putting themselves out or even taking you on a path unconnected to your project - you still run with it. As a result there are many experiences and people I met along the way and while not actually included in this book, they have been an integral part of the project.

This is particularly evident in the large number of encounters and stories I received from my visits to the local primary school in Skryne. Child after child came to me with stories and accounts they had heard, some new and contemporary, while others had been passed on or heard (and mis-heard) from family and friends. It always excites me to hear a story which has existed in a particular family, a townland or the wider village, decades or even centuries after the incident occurred. Apart from the usual stories that children have heard and read about Tara, there were many unofficial or locally told stories concerning the site, like the men who shot the fingers off the old St. Patrick statue and the supposed bad luck they got. So, it's only natural that the more stories people have, either personal accounts or shared community stories, the more connected to the place they feel.

Since the 1950s and 60s there has been a huge shift in how people live in rural Ireland. Those who have moved out from our towns and cities often simply want a bigger house and to live in the countryside. In addition to this, the new generations of country people have slowly become disconnected from the fields, ditches and gaps which surround them due to the shifts in their own ways of life. I acknowledge this shift, and although it pains me to see what has been lost, coming from a coastal farming/fishing community myself, this type of project is not necessarily about preserving these stories or ways of life. Instead I see it as a means of re-framing and re-presenting what we still have, as well as generating new conversations about this place, helping people connect and ultimately siting them physically and mentally in the place in which they live.

People's experience's of Tara have widened and developed for a variety of reasons; family, community, personal, touristic, recreational, commercial, spiritual, cultural, historical and environmental. In my encounters I have met people who connect with the site on many of these different levels, some for quiet, personal reasons, while others are as part of a communal experience, some ancient in practice and others contemporary. It's all here and this particular project does not intend to encapsulate everything, it is just some captured moments from people at a particular place and time. I feel that Tara will always have stories. The site demands the attention of people and it needs them as much as the people need it. I feel this is the way it has always been and always will be.

'Your Tara, My Tara', Michael Fortune, June 2014.

Foreword

Tara has been an assembly point and sacred site central to Irish history, life and lore for many millennia. Its name is synonymous with high-kings, as a sanctuary of prehistoric, pre-Christian and early medieval Ireland and a powerful symbol of political sovereignty and freedom at the heart of Irish national identity. This sense of connection and continuity is very strong and is reflected in people's attachment to, and love of, this special place.

Michael Fortune has undertaken a participative public art project by engaging with people who live near or visit Tara to explore what this special place means to them and how it has shaped their sense of place. Michael's engaging personality and style shine through the pages of My Tara.

My Tara is a collaborative project between the Heritage and Arts Offices of Meath County Council. Continuing on the success of previous 'My Tara' collaborations, Meath County Council is proud to be at the forefront of support for artists and their work in contemporary Meath. Our shared commitment to creating meaningful experiences for our citizens paves the way to promoting participation in and access to arts and heritage in the future.

We would like to thank Michael Fortune for his engaging approach to this project and to all the staff and pupils of Scoil Cholmcille National School in Skryne who so willingly participated. We would like to acknowledge the support of local residents and visitors to Tara and OPW staff (past and present) who contributed their stories and reflections of Tara. Particular acknowledgement is due to the Arts Council and Heritage Council for their financial support towards this project and for their ongoing support in the implementation of our Arts and Heritage Programme.

My Tara explores, and helps us to understand, the relationship between a community and its landscape.

Cllr Jim Holloway
Cathaoirleach Meath County Council

Jackie Maguire
Chief Executive, Meath County Council

Opposite: Meath Arts Office Dawn Chorus May 2013 celebrating Bealtaine Festival

St. Patrick's Fingers	11
My People, My Place	17
Visitor's Book	23
False Windows	27
Signs	31
Maurice and Michael	37
Memories of '98	43
The Dodie Tree	49
When the Landscape Changes	55
Good Luck	61
Small Country	67
The Energy Fields	73
Fire	81
Light and Dark	85
Biography	93
Acknowledgements	95

St. Patrick's Fingers

St. Patrick has had a long association with the Hill of Tara. Towards the end of the nineteenth century, a statue of the saint was erected on the hill to commemorate Patrick lighting a fire on the nearby Hill of Slane on the eve of Easter Sunday, around 433 AD. While more claim that the statue was erected on what is actually a 'Croppies' grave' from 1798 and that its erection coincided with the 1798 Centenary Commemorations. The statue, by Navan sculptor Thomas Curry, has suffered a number of injuries since its creation, mostly notably when it was peppered with gunshots resulting in the loss of its fingers and part of its hand. This particular story, part of local folklore to this day, even made an appearance in the 'Schools Folklore Scheme' (1937-38) where it was recounted by local children. As to be expected, stories abound about the bad luck suffered by the shooters and accounts of these are still murmured.

Apart from the pot-shots of some gun men, the statue was also the target of relic hunters and before its removal, small bits and pieces were chipped away by visitors to the hill. In 1992 it was removed by the Office of Public Works (OPW) for refurbishment. I met with one of the men who was part of the removal team in 1992, and he told me of its removal in the dark of night. There was outrage locally following its removal, and in October 1996 a new statue was commissioned after a selection process. However, the work by Cork-born artist Annette Hennessy of an eight-foot bronze statue which depicted Patrick as a young boy, dressed as a swine herdsman, never saw the hill after much local and national debate. It even reached the chambers of the Dáil in March 1997 and following these debates a more traditional statue of Patrick was sourced and erected on the hill, where it remains.

I was curious to see if I could find out more information on the original statue which had been removed. What state was it in, had it been refurbished, or even if it was still in existence at all? I began my enquiries, and found that it was the belief of many local people that the statue had been destroyed. Articles written at the time of its removal perpetuated this myth as they exaggerate the damage it suffered during dismantling and storage. However, after some calls and emails, I was taken by two OPW workers to a workshop in Trim where St. Patrick stands solitary in the corner, quietly redundant, awaiting his destiny. While his injuries are plain to see, I found him to be in far better repair than I'd imagined. I wondered if perhaps he might yet return to the hill from which he came? Accommodated in the Visitor's Centre locals and visitors could reconnect with him and perhaps record the various stories associated with the statue.

My Great Grand father buried some coins When the british isRealites were looking for the Ork of the covenent My Great Grand father shot the fingers off the Statue of St. patrick.

by Lucy

Opposite: Statue of St. Patrick, OPW Depot, Trim, Co. Meath (October 2013)
Above: Story written by Lucy Wilkinson, Skryne NS, Skryne, Co. Meath (February 2013)

Opposite and above: St. Patrick with wooden hand in the OPW Depot, Trim, Co. Meath (October 2013)

My People, My Place

Tara holds a special place in many hearts and minds. This naturally includes many people from the locality. One such person I met was Dan McCabe from nearby Garlow Cross. When I met Dan, he told me that "We always hear that it takes the "blow-in" or the outsider to make us realise what we have, but I didn't, I always knew here was special".

I'd been in contact with Dan following an email from his daughter Martha in March. Martha had outlined how important the hill is to her father and family. Dan was recovering from a recent illness and maybe his mind was in a contemplative state. On a fine summer day, Dan met me in the car park and our first point of interest was Mairéad Carew's book, *Tara and the Ark of the Covenant* which he'd brought along to show me. Standing by his car, he pointed out from photos in the book, his own local relatives who had been employed by the British Israelites to dig on the hill for the Ark of the Covenant between 1899 and 1902. Back then, as he alludes, this was work in a hard-pressed Ireland of the time.

Dan walked me to the graveyard. As in any rural village or community, the graveyard is a great leveller. As we are aware, many people visit the hill for a variety and combination of reasons: archaeological, historical, leisure, touristic and spiritual. However, the graveyard on the Hill of Tara is one of those places that connects people physically and spiritually to the site. It's a place where family members and friends can go to spend quiet moments with those who have passed and gone.

The ground was a carpet of daisies. As we moved from grave to grave Dan spelled out the engraved names of his family members, friends and neighbours and recounted stories about their lives. He settled on the line of headstones belonging to his own family and pointed to where he will be buried. Death comes to us all and it seems that Dan finds solace in knowing that his final resting place will be on the Hill of Tara.

Michael Fortune <mytaraproject@gmail.com>

My Tara

Martha McCabe @gmail.com> Thu, Mar 21, 2013 at 11:54 AM
To: mytaraproject@gmail.com

Hi Michael

I have heard of your project and I think it is fantastic. Below is my story. It may not be relevant and I won't be able to send you pictures until I visit my parents and get copies x

The Hill of Tara and my Family.

As a child the Hill of Tara was always seen as 'home'. Every weekend, every special occasion was mark with a trip to the hill of Tara. My older brothers and sister, me, and my younger siblings have all and still do enjoy the spoils of Tara.

Our history with the Hill of Tara began with my dad. Born and bread in Walterstown he used to work Barney Norton at the end of the lane by Reilly's cottage. Dad would regale us with stories of how, when he was bored or need 'me' time he would walk the fields up to the hill of Tara,sit overlooking Dalgan and count his money, not a lot, but he re counted and recounted. My dad's heart belongs to Tara and it always will. When my dad first met my mam, a Liverpool girl, he used to walk her his familys new home, the Garlow Cross Post Office (My grandmother being the post mistress for the area) up to the hill of Tara for romantic walks. Perhaps it was the beauty of Tara that made them fall more in love but they married soon after meeting and in 1978 they welcomed my older sister. They called her Tara. Some of my sisters first days on earth were spent living with my dad's brother at the bottom of the Hill of Tara in a cottage they were living in.

In 1980 my older brother John was born. John was named after my dad's best friend who past away tragically but is buried in his family plot in the Hill of Tara's graveyard. The graveyard of the Hill of Tara is as precious a sanctuary and the Hill itself. Buried in this graveyard are my great grandparents, my grandfather Patrick (my dad's dad) , my great aunts and uncles and my 2 uncles, Thomas and Michael, taken all too suddenly. My dad often takes trips to their graves and find solice in the surroundings being able to speak with his brothers.

I was born in 1986 and our love affair with the Hill continued. All of my childhood snaps are of me playing on the hill with cousins and friends or of me enjoying the snow capped hills, skidding down atop coal bags or in home made sleighs! Snow days were always best spent at Tara!

The Hill of Tara has often been the subject of many a funny story in our home, be it the story of the time my father counted his money and hid it buried in one of the sloped banks on the hill of Tara so his brothers wouldn't take it and then forgetting where it was (eventually found) or to my brother deciding to celebrate his stag party in his birthday suit running round the Mound of The Hostages under a full mood only to discover he'd lost his car keys and couldn't get back to his clothes!

All generations of my family young and old have held Tara dear. In 1998 & 2000 we welcomed Patrick and Maeve to our family. The younger of my siblings. My mam and dad chose Maeve's name after my dad took a walk through Tara on a day he was feeling quite down. My mam has been very ill in hospital whilst pregnant and I was at home, 13 years old, caring for my baby brother as my older siblings worked. My dad had left the hospital and decided to take a walk through the Hill to clear his

mind. On his walk he came across Rath Maeve. a sense of relief came over him as he sat there and a few days later my little sister arrived and my mam's health recovered. Maeve was chosen as her name because she was as beautiful as the surrounds where her name came into consideration.

their childhoods were as blessed as mine to have been spent playing on The Hill. Even today, looking out my parents window, you can see the hill shining bright. My parents live in Gerrardstown, close to Garlow Cross and our home is called 'Tara View'.. as you can tell alot of our life revolves around Tara.

From personal experience I have always found peace at the Hill. Whenever I am upset or down I take a trip there and find the peace I need to clear my head. The Hill of Tara is more than a tourist spot or a beautiful walk, it is a second home to all who have grown to love this amazing place. This is a place I know that for now, and when I am long gone will be engraved in our family history. Family and friends have been buried here and our families footsteps have shapped these hills for many years. Tara is a place we can proudly bring our friends and family to as say this is home, this is Meath, this is heaven.

Even sitting atop the Hill looking over the landscape I can see our Dalgan College, a college my great grandfather helped build, where he met his future wife who began my great grandmother. A place my grandfather work, my uncles work and met their wives, I can see the old post office my grandmother used to run and where my father spent his childhood years. I can see my own home, a place I spend the happiest years of my life. The Hill of Tara represents not only a community of people who have loved this spot for generations but it represents memories. The wind on the Hill carries with it the laughter of ages and the memories of days spent with loved ones.

Opposite: Email from Martha McCabe (March 2013)
Above: Graveyard, Hill of Tara, Co. Meath (May 2013)

Opposite: Seat erected by the McCabe family for the late Michael 'Mickey' McCabe
Above: Dan McCabe points to his family headstones in the graveyard on Tara (May 2013)

Hill of Tara
Teamhair

Guides 1991

1. Gerard Clarke
2. Mark Mulvey
3. Gráinne Hamill
4. Fíona Dowling
5. Peter Crinion

1992

1. Gerard Clarke
2. Mark Mulvey
3. Gráinne Hamill
4. Carol Smith

Visitor Centre Opened Oct - 1992

1993

1. Gerard Clarke
2. Joan Rogers
3. Mark Mulvey
4. Lara Jenkins
5. Linda Fitzsimons

1994

1. Gerard Clarke

1995

1. Gerard Clarke

1996

1. Lara Jenkins

Visitor's Book

When working as OPW tour guides on the hill in the 1990s, Ger Clarke and his fellow guides made a concerted effort to get any visitors with the Christian name Tara to sign their name in the Visitor's Book. When I met Ger he told me the story but was unsure where the book was - probably still in the centre, he said. After some calls, I was handed the book by Joan Revington, OPW Head Guide at Tara.

The use of the girl's name 'Tara' reached a peak in the 1970s in the USA, having become popular as a result of the use of the name in the novel and subsequent film *Gone with the Wind*. Tara was the name given to the Plantation in the novel and subsequent film. Apart from leaving a lasting influence on people's names throughout the world, the name Tara is also the name of Dolly Parton's mansion in Nashville, Tennessee.

On opening the book it was apparent that the Hill of Tara was the destination of many people with the name, and that they got a great deal of satisfaction and enjoyment out of visiting the place which had given them their name. Tara Dippel from California declared 'I'm home', while Tara Rice from New York wrote 'I'm so happy to finally see the place I'm named after and it's beautiful'.

The names of the OPW guides from that time were neatly written in pen, in tables drawn with a ruler and ballpoint pen, at the beginning of the book. These days such information would no doubt be typed up and printed out, but this more personal and physical writing appealed to me. Flicking through the pages as the book fills up and the tour guides changed, the intense concentration of the name Tara disappears as the years pass on. I'm delighted that this effort was made by those guides to record these visits, creating another lovely layer of experience to the history of the site.

Date	Name	Location	Comment
29/94	Tara Corrigan Hicksville, N.Y.		Home again T.G.!!
7/94			
/94	Alan Barrett		
/94	Tara Mathieson		Cold + Raining but beautiful
4	Tara Watson Melbourne, Australia		Lovely just like our Tara
4	Christopher & Lynn		No need to comment! Excellent
4	Tara carty		Laindon
	Jonathan, Kath Miraflores, Lima, Peru		The guides are incredulous!
	Frank Lodwidge, Liverpool		
	Tara Sullivan, New York		
	Tara Quigley		Rugby England age 5.
	Paddy Fitzmaurice		Meath Co.C.
	TARA MAguire		LAndon
	Tara Michelle Conway		Boston, USA age 21
	Paula Bycroft - Beyond 2000		Australia - Spectacular
	Sean O'Carroll		Dunshaughlin
	Daithí Ó hÓgáin		UCD
	Ryland Hogan		
	Calvi Vekeben		Norfolk, England.
	Tara Ingalls		Petaluma, California
	Jerry & Jane Burroni		San Anselmo, California
	Marie Rahilly		Wickham Rd, Harrow Wea

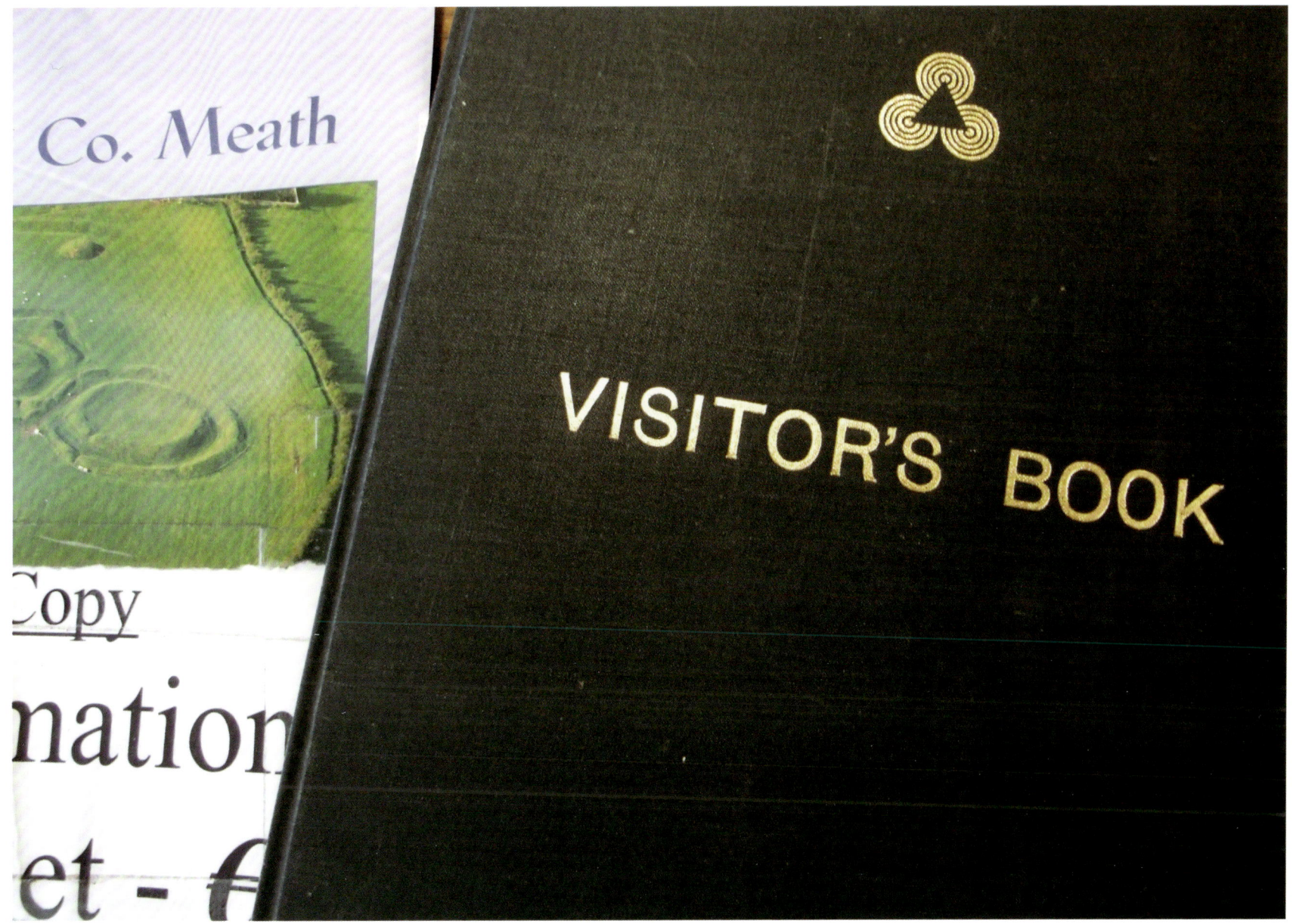

Opposite: Page from Visitor's Book (1994), Visitor's Centre, Hill of Tara, Co. Meath (June 2013)
Above: Cover of old Visitor's Book, Visitor's Centre, Hill of Tara, Co. Meath (June 2013)

False Windows

The Church on Tara has been deceiving people for years. Outwardly it presents itself as a classic stone building, with tall narrow windows on each side and a stained-glass feature window on the altar end. Though I had visited the church on a couple of occasions it wasn't until Ger Clarke pointed a detail out to me that I realised that its interior doesn't match how it is presented externally.

Ger told me that the present church was rebuilt (c. 1822) beside the ruins of an earlier fourteenth-century church. (The outline of the old church is still visible in the graveyard). During its construction, no windows or openings were incorporated in the north wall. Curiously, cut-stone window frames were manufactured and installed, but the openings were rendered solid. On the inside the wall runs continuously with no visible sign of the frame or opening. The architectural conceit at the time was to not have any doors or windows on a building's north face. However, in order to maintain architectural symmetry, windows were sometimes alluded to - as in this case at Tara. Whether this was an exercise to ward off evil spirits or simply a practical attempt to keep out the cold, we don't know.

Opposite and above: Visitor's Centre, Hill of Tara, Co. Meath (May 2013)

Signs

Growing up, my nickname was 'Lethuse'. This arose after my own father, selling lettuce from our home, erected a home-made sign "Lethuse for Sale". The upshot of this was that from the first day of secondary school some months later I became known as 'Lethuse'. As a result, many people in my home and neighbouring villages are still unsure of my first name and awkwardly greet me as 'Lethuse, sorry Mick…Michael isn't it?' when we bump into each other decades later.

It's not surprising then that unusual signs capture my attention. Whether professional, home-made, permanent or temporary, signs have the potential to be purely informative, misread, obeyed, disobeyed, or in some cases, bring a smile to your face.

A sign saying "No Camping" certainly gets the message across that camping here is not allowed, but it also suggests that this place might be a nice site to camp if someone went to the bother of erecting a sign discouraging it.

LADIES

Enter for Tearooms

Opposite: Temporary signs, Hill of Tara, Co. Meath (April 2013)
Above: Temporary dwellings, Hill of Tara, Co. Meath (June 2013)

Old Book Shop OPEN
the old book shop
michael slavin
author
the book of tara
Old Book Shop

Maurice and Michael

I'd heard about the bookshop on the Hill of Tara long before I ever visited. When the opportunity to undertake this project came up I instantly resolved to make it one of my first stops. The shop is owned and run by Michael Slavin helped out by Maurice Cassidy who lives across the road with his wife Mary. If you Google any history of Tara, undoubtedly Michael Slavin's name comes up. Mention to anyone you are doing a project on Tara and they all say 'You should talk to Michael Slavin'. Apart from his own knowledge and experience, the bookshop is an incredible depository of printed material, ancient and contemporary, set in a small shed-like building on the side of the hill. Michael's keen eye for the unusual and culturally important makes this shop unique. It's like walking into someone's personal library, but in this case you can take away his books, for a small fee.

Maurice was tending to the shop on my first few visits to the Hill. Maurice's wife is from near where I live in County Wexford and we'd a common link right away. When I met Michael for the first time some months later I felt a little awkward at meeting a man who has spent most of his adult life working and living the Tara experience. How could I possibly capture what he knows and relate his experience of Tara? I couldn't. Instead I'll tell you of my experience with the two men. Maurice and Michael have a relationship based on mutual and comedic disregard for each other's actions or feelings. Maurice recounted the time he was building a wall across from the shop, leading down to his own house. Michael, he says, would sit 'on his arse' on a chair outside the front door of the shop, 'passing comment' on every stone he laid in the wall.

During one of my visits Maurice walked into the shop and threw a comment about Michael 'guntering away' with a book. Not knowing the term, they both explained it as meaning clever, inventive and improvised labour-saving tools and techniques. In this particular case Michael was guntering at old books with a pencil, removing past writing, a sticker and so on. Maurice went on to tell me about the time when Michael bought a sledge post driver and Maurice and his friend, not impressed with this new contraption, went about putting down a stake in sight of Michael, with one man holding the stake driver on the stake and the other hitting it with a sledge. Needless to say, this was a deliberate misunderstanding for their own enjoyment in a bid to torment Michael, who as expected, rushed to tell them they were doing it wrong.

I left the shop after chatting about loads of things that could have featured in this book, like how at the time of the papal visit to Ireland in 1979 a local priest and some parishioners had cut the papal symbol into the grass in the hope that Pope John Paul II would see it as he flew over. It was foggy and he didn't. But mostly I think of the time when I was preparing to leave after a long chat with Maurice in the shop, and he mentioned about clampers being outside. So, I quickly packed up and rushed back to my car, only to realise I'd been had.

INVESTING IN GEORGIAN GLASS
ENCYCLOPEDIA PRACTICAL PHOTOGRAPHY
TARA
Ireland

Opposite: Michael Slavin 'guntering' in his bookshop, Hill of Tara, Co. Meath (October 2013)
Above: Painting of Tara village, The Old Book Shop, Hill of Tara, Co. Meath (October 2013)

Irish houses & castles
Brian Boru
King of Ireland
POBLACHT NA H EIREANN
THE PROVISIONAL GOVERNMENT
IRISH REPUBLIC
TO THE PEOPLE OF IRELAND
Ray-Ban
Photographs
TARA
HILL OF HEROES
IRELAND
BOB DYLAN
COLLECTION TWO
Battle of the Boyne
1690
Der Tara-
Rundgang
THE
TARA
WALK
IRISH WRITERS

Opposite: Maurice Cassidy in The Old Book Shop, Hill of Tara, Co. Meath (January 2013)
Above: Maurice Cassidy holds 'a tool for guntering' in The Old Book Shop, Hill of Tara, Co. Meath (October 2013)

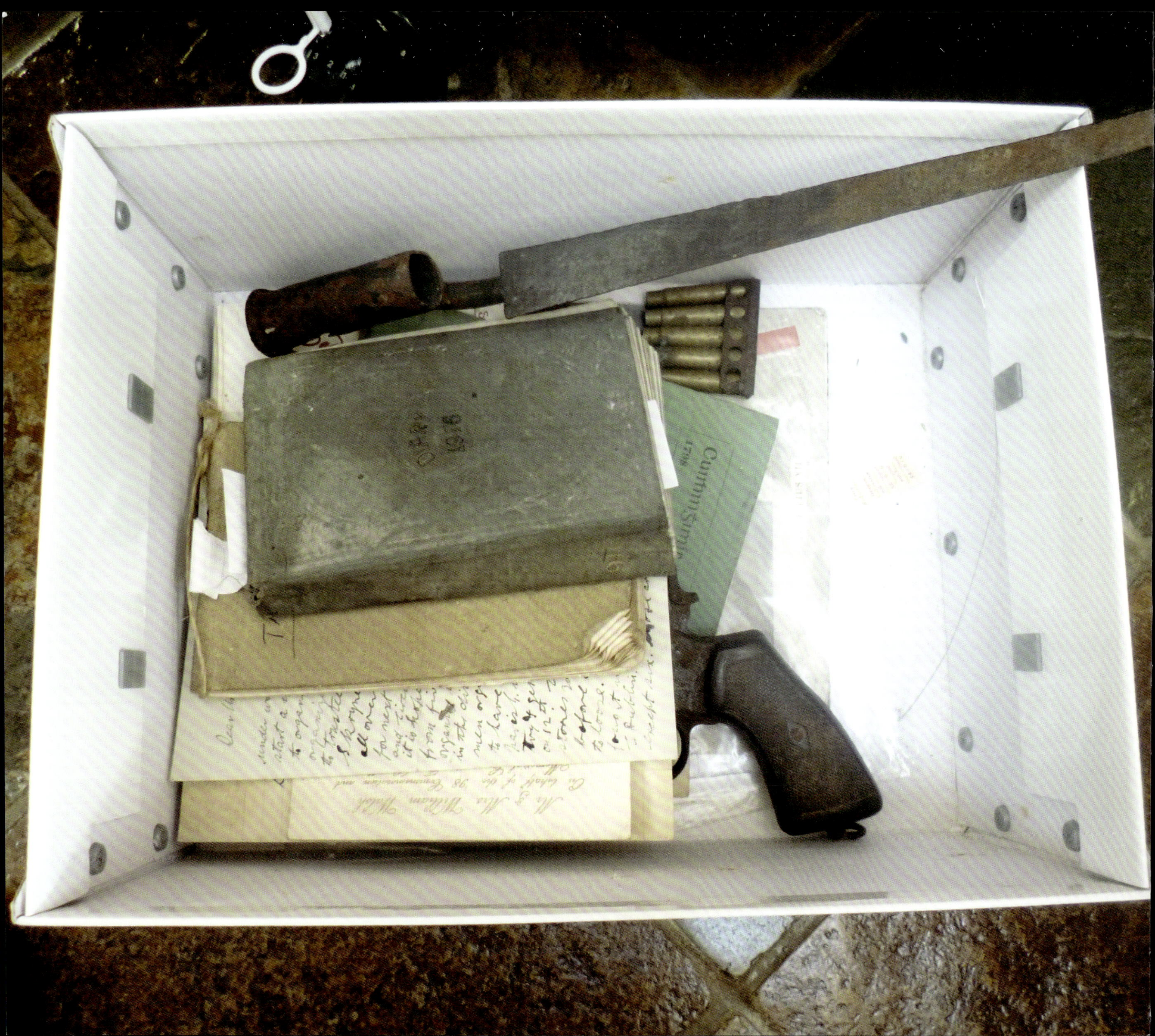
DIARY 1916

Memories of '98

1798 was a turbulent time in Irish history and it too left its mark on the Hill of Tara. On the 26th of May 1798 the Battle of Tara took place when United Irishmen and rebels from Meath and neighbouring counties took up position on the hill. However, they could not compete with the better-armed Fencible, Yeoman and Militia forces and the rebels were suppressed.

A month later in Wexford, the United Irishmen and rebels were defeated on Vinegar Hill, and in a last bid attempt to join their northern counterparts, they marched north with fellow Croppies from Wicklow and Carlow into Meath and north Co. Dublin. Although there were various battles and skirmishes involving Wexford rebels in Meath, there is still debate whether any were involved in a later battle on the Hill of Tara.

Following a contact with someone regarding something completely different, I met with Richard Farrelly from Balgeeth in Kilmessan, who has a love for history and place. After a few conversations on the phone, I called around to have a general chat about Tara. After a few hours of excited talking about various things of interest, he disappeared down the hall and came back with a cardboard box with '1798' and '1916' written on it. He placed it on the floor and lifted the lid. It was like opening a treasure trove: full of old letters, papers, newspaper cuttings, programmes and notebooks. Most striking in this was a rusty revolver from the 1916/War of Independence period, and a British Brown Bess Bayonet. Richard was told by his grandfather that three Murrays had fought in the Battle of Tara: two were killed and one returned home with this bayonet. On close inspection we identified the maker's name (Dawes) and some markings. From subsequent research into military records based on production markings, we found that the bayonet matches the exact period.

Richard's own grandfather was a central figure in the 150th Commemoration in Meath and was central to the erection of the 1798 monument that currently stands on the hill. As we chatted he kept producing letters, minutes and speech notes from the time: hand-written notes from meetings in Skyrne, letters from organisers from Wexford and notes on an IRA firing party. One remarkable set of notebooks belonging to his grandfather emerged: these featured notes in relation to known graves of Croppies and specific accounts from 1798, which in 1948 one must remember, was not long out of living memory.

On departing Richard gave me one of his original copies of the programme of events from the event in Tara in 1948, which I will treasure dearly.

cuimnigimís ar 1798
Coiste Cuimneacáin na m...
i dTeamair

Brochure

Commemorative of those who f...
on the Hill of Tara...
freedom of Meath in
parts of...

Ceremonies o...

...NDAY, 3rd...

4 Irish Times ... 1952

THE STORY OF TARA

II—THE EAR... YEARS

WE have told briefly the sto...
these manuscripts come the...
been recited in that very ban...
They have been told and re-tol...
and Raths and houses and ...
and legends and histori...
for any but the spe...
is legend : the ...
reflect a civ...
heirs.

COMMEMORATION
Cuimnigimis ar '98
(ASSOCIATION)

Ramsgrange:— ...
M. Mac Eochaidh, O.S., ...
Wexford.

Opposite: Letters, printed material and bayonet, Richard Farrelly's house, Balgeeth, Kilmessan, Co. Meath (September 2013)
Above: Richard Farrelly holds newspaper cuttings from his grandfather's 1798 archive, Balgeeth, Kilmessan, Co. Meath (September 2013)

Book 1

TARA 1798

R.J. MURRAY
KILMESSAN

4th Oct '48 Monday
Met Mr Woods Blacksmith Bolies,
Duleek at Barbers Navan

Story
Three Wexford men called at farmers house named Morgan who lived in house opposite well of Deens (North Side). Footsore and weary got food and bed on hurdle. Morgan went to Dillon of Manninstown Yeoman captain to inform. Yeos came. Prodded men through hurdle. One young man oversize feet jumped through window (Probably the built up window) was pursued + shot in stomach. Jumped backwards 20 feet. Asked for drink which ran out. Next morning the sow was found eating intestines. This mans widowed mother came all...

(Page missing. Story ends. More than likely would have read that she came all 'the way from Wexford to recover or bury her dead son'.)

Notes taken by R.J. Murray, Kilmessan in the lead up to the 150th Year Commeration of the 1798 Rebellion on the Hill of Tara and Co. Meath. One of a series of books that is held by Richard Farrelly, Balgeeth, Kilmessan, Co. Meath (September 2013)

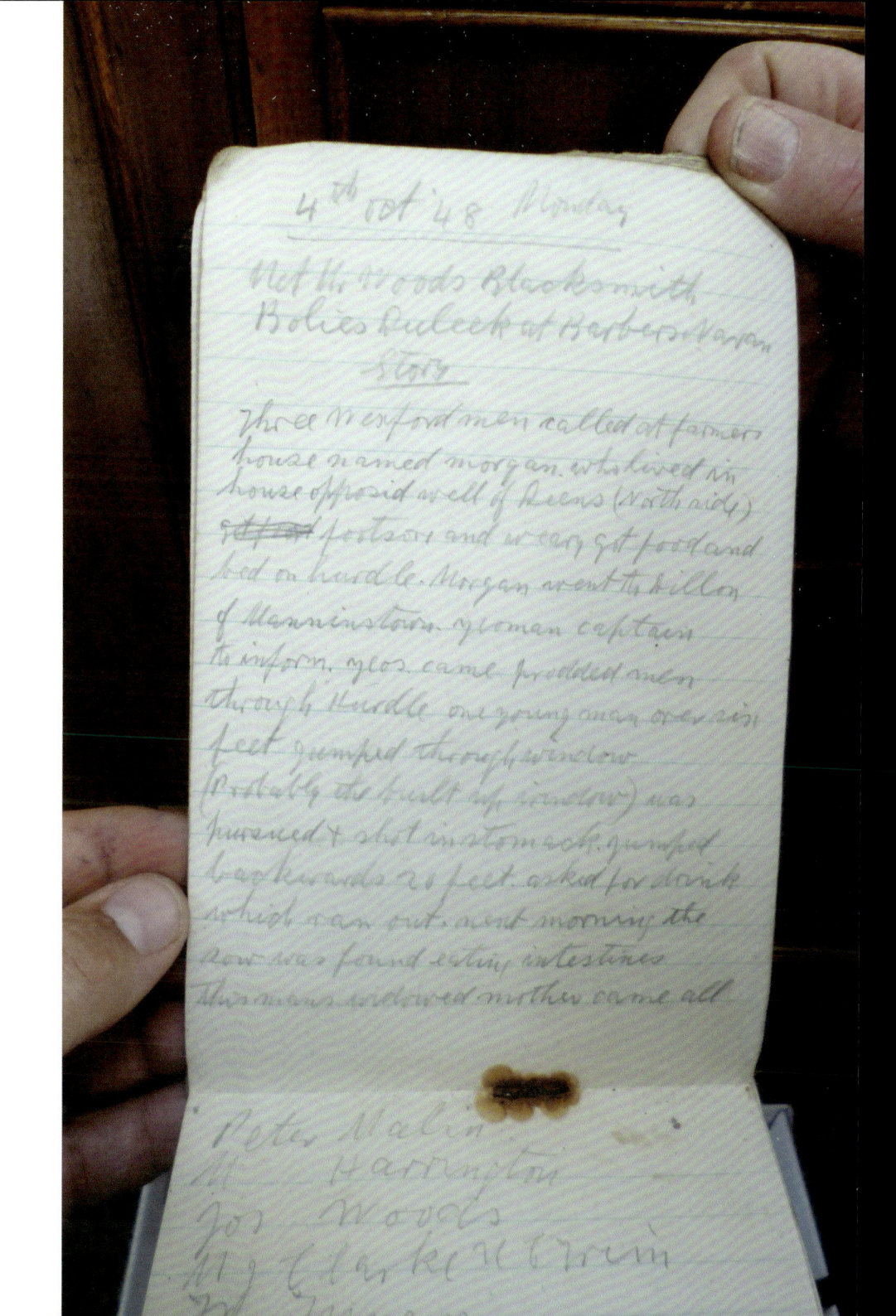

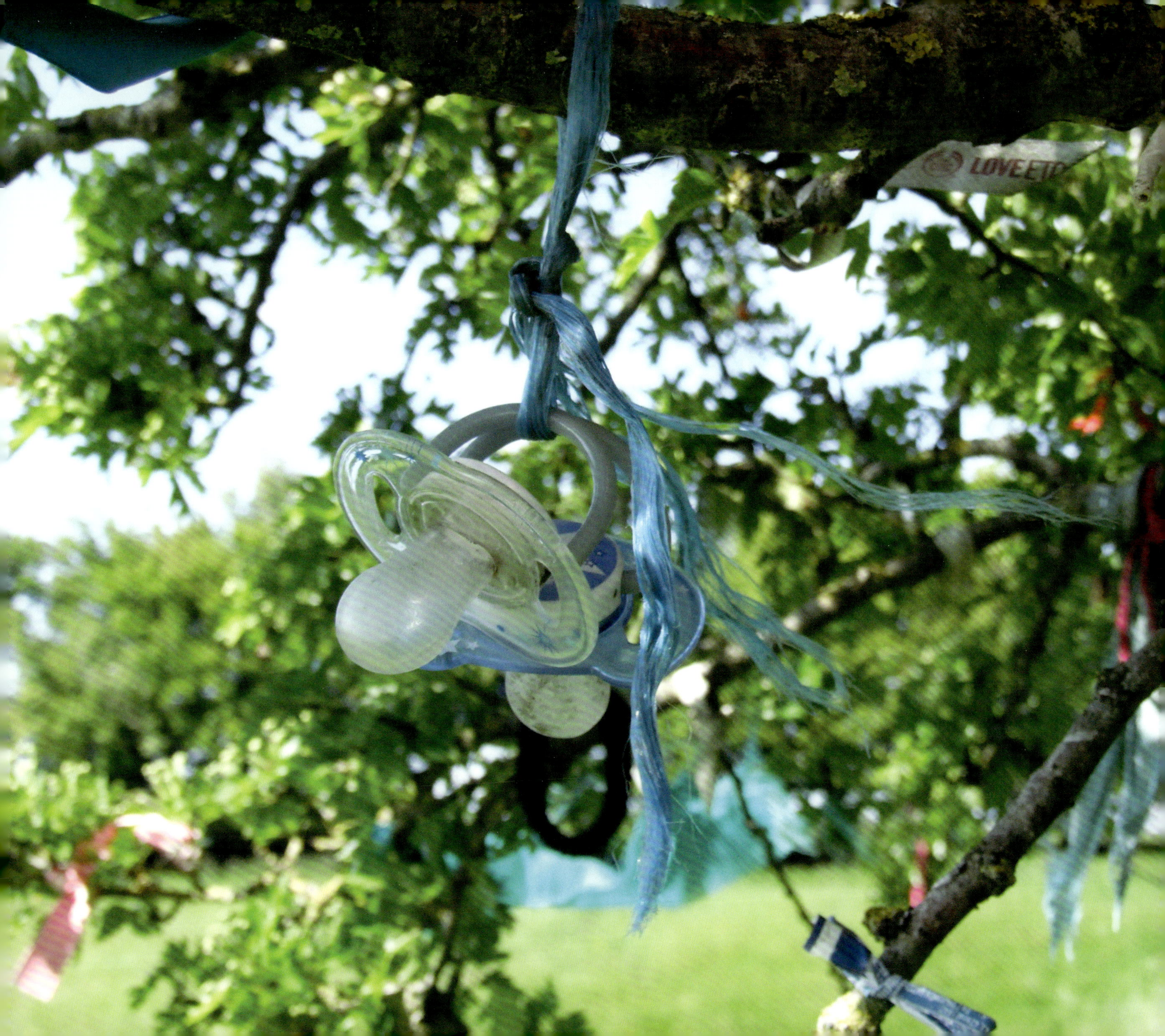

The Dodie Tree

In recent years local toddlers tie their dodies (dudie, soothers or dummies) onto the double rag tree on the hill when they (or their parents) wish to give them up. Traditionally rag trees were used by people to make a wish or leave a prayer, with people leaving small pieces of clothing, ribbons, medals, coins, crutches and other such objects on the boughs of the tree. The tradition of decorating this particular tree is relatively recent, with an older rag tree being located at a different site on the hill. However, the act of placing children's dodies on the tree seems to have taken off and more and more toddlers are brought to the hill for one of their first big challenges in life.

Another story I encountered in relation to the dodie was sent to me by Jill Jacob and her daughter Aaliyah who took a different approach to the custom: they tied the dodie to a helium balloon and let go. I know this would probably make the task even more difficult for my own three-year-old daughter who is currently equally very fond of both her own dodie and helium balloons. I wouldn't be confident of a positive result from such an exercise!

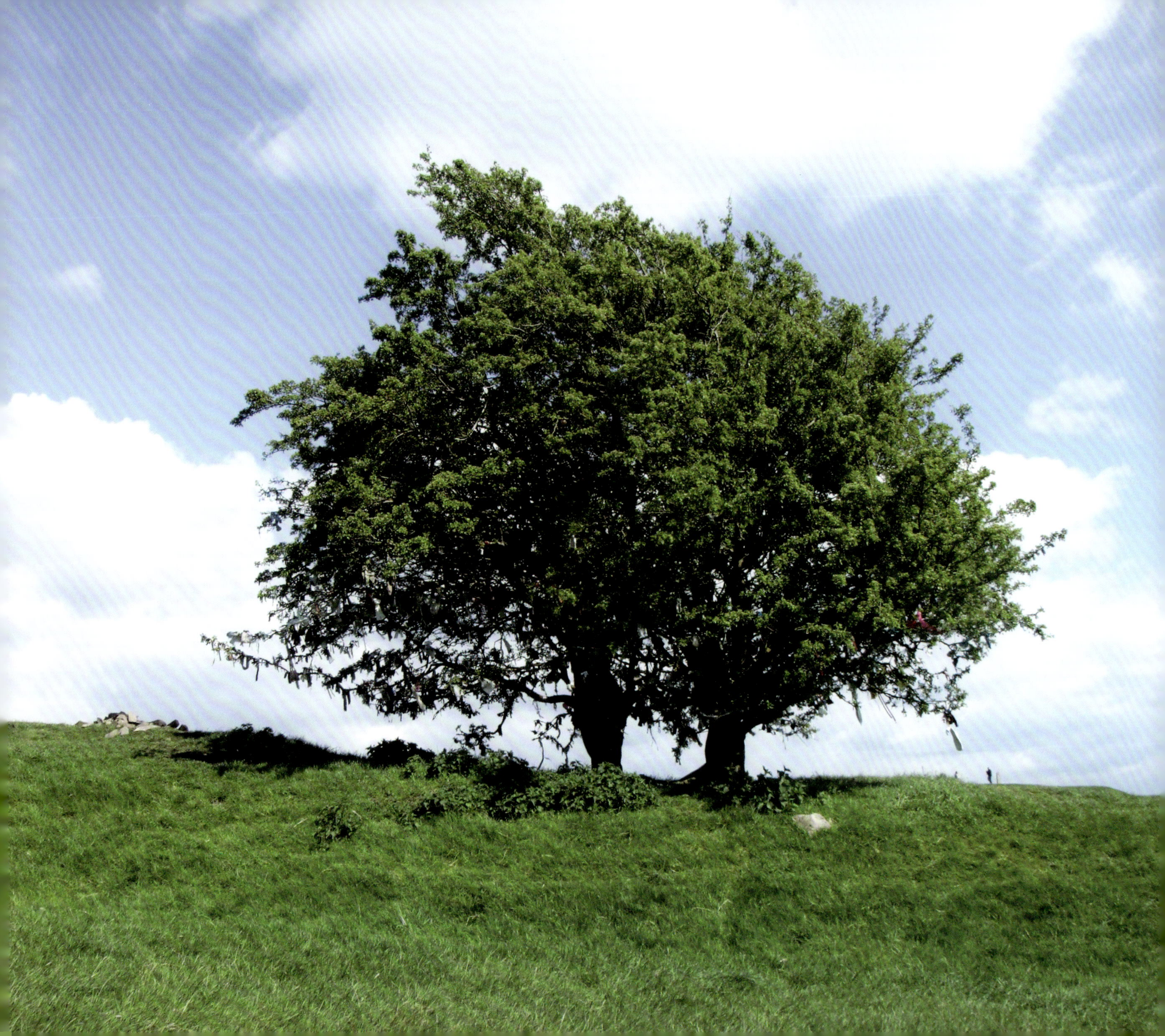

Opposite and above: The Dodie Tree, Hill of Tara, Co. Meath (April 2013)

Tara Hill

My Memory of Tara Hill is about the dudie fairy's.
I was four years old.
I went there with my Mom and Dad.
We had a small picnic.
Mom explained to me that the
fairy's in Tara Hill take dudie's from
girls and give them to little
babies who need them.
After our picnic we tied my
favourite pink dudie to a balloon and
sent it off to the fairy's in the sky
over Tara Hill.
I still miss my dudie very much.

The End

Aaliyah age seven

Above: Jill, Mark, Aaliyah and baby Zach Jacob, Hill of Tara, Co. Meath (Summer 2010)
Opposite: Story written by Aaliyah Jacob (June 2013)

Photos taken on mobile phone by Jill and Mark Jacob

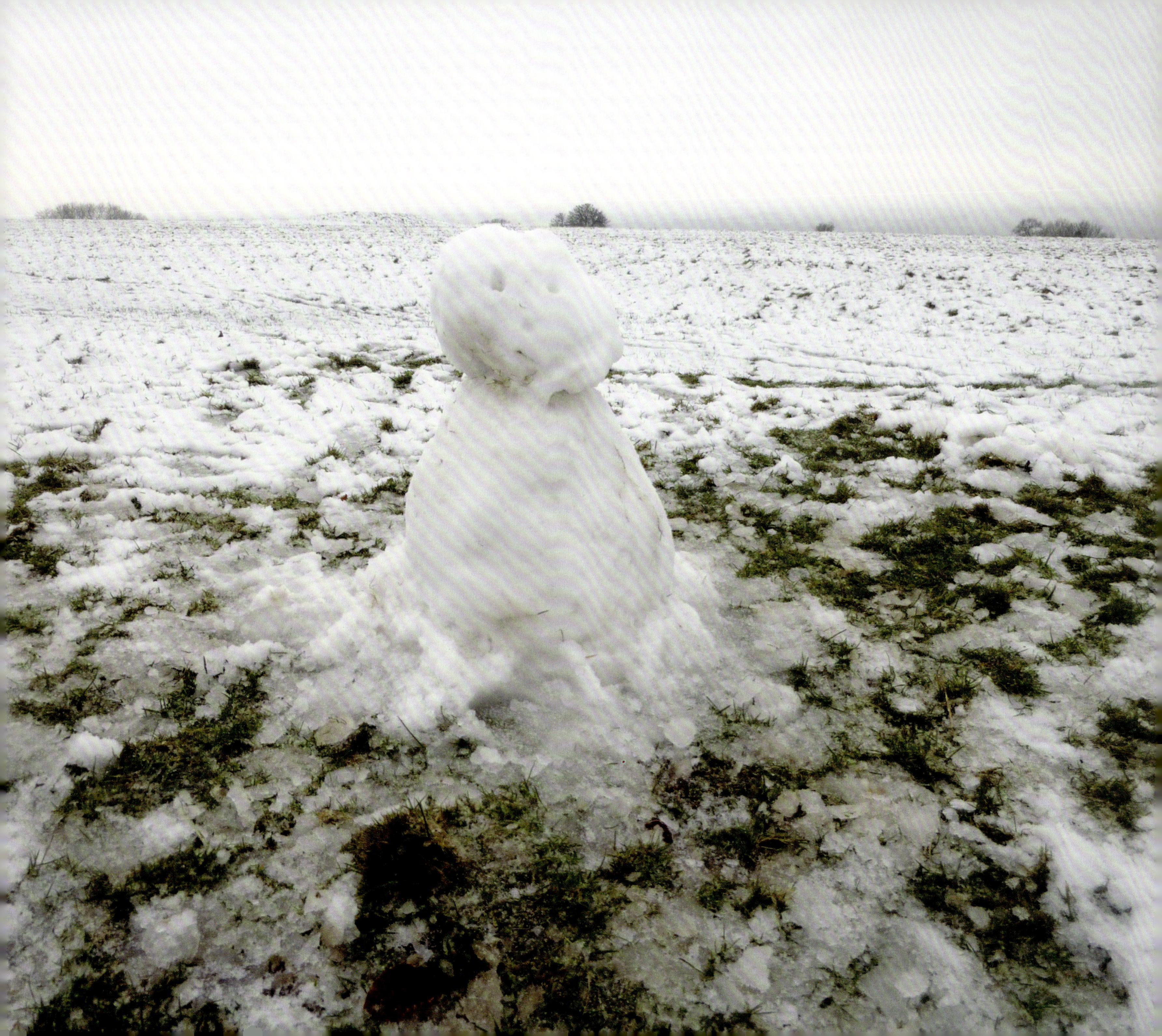

When the Landscape Changes

On a fine day, Tara attracts its fair share of walkers and runners alike. Combine the attraction of the hill with the white stuff and it is every child's wonderland.

A few hours of building snowmen and buzzing up and down the sloping banks of the hill leaves every child wanting the comfort of the famous mug of hot chocolate available from Maguires next door. Every child I spoke to in the school in Skryne maintains it's a necessary part of any visit to the hill. It'd be 'like going to mass and not getting communion' one child told me. Stories abound about the antics on the hill in the snow. 'Go to YouTube and type in Snow Tara' I was told. 'Honestly - it's class'.

It's amazing how inventive we can become when we want a thrill. When I was younger we used a plastic bag filled with straw, not that you'd have been surprised to see the bonnet of a car used as a sledge. Now the lid of a roof box or a surf board are as likely to be seen.

Hill Of Tara Project

My story today that I will share with you is about the big snow in 2010. Every day we went up to the Hill of Tara to go sledding. After we went into the cafe to get a hot chocolate with marshmallows. The roads were so snowy cars weren't able to drive that well only jeeps and tractors. One day when we were going up a sheep was in our way. The snow was so deep that his bum was wiggling up and down but he blended in with the scenery so all we could see was his legs wiggling up and down.

Another story I would like to tell you is about my brother and my friend's mum. My brother was sliding down and my Friend's mum was coming up the hill and when he was going down he bumped in to her she fell over and got a small cut up above her eyebrow. The two of them were on the ground covered in snow laughing and crying at the same time it was hard to tell because it was so funny. That day there were lots of different things that people used to slid on the snow here is a list of things that we saw, Car bonnet turned upside down, an old surfboard, an empty paddling pool for kids, old election posters, homemade toboggans, one man was on a pair of skis. We had empty fertilizer bags which were the fastest and slippiest of all. We started at the back of the Hill close to the Fairy Tree near the sloping trenches. We slid all the way down and then had to walk slowly back up to slide all the way back down again. (trying to keep out of the way of the other people sliding down). That's my stories and fun memories from the Hill of Tara and I hopped you have enjoyed reading them!

Opposite: Accounts from Caragh Conway via her father's email address (September 2013)
Above: Photo taken by Caragh Conway from 'The Big Snow of 2010', Hill of Tara, Co. Meath

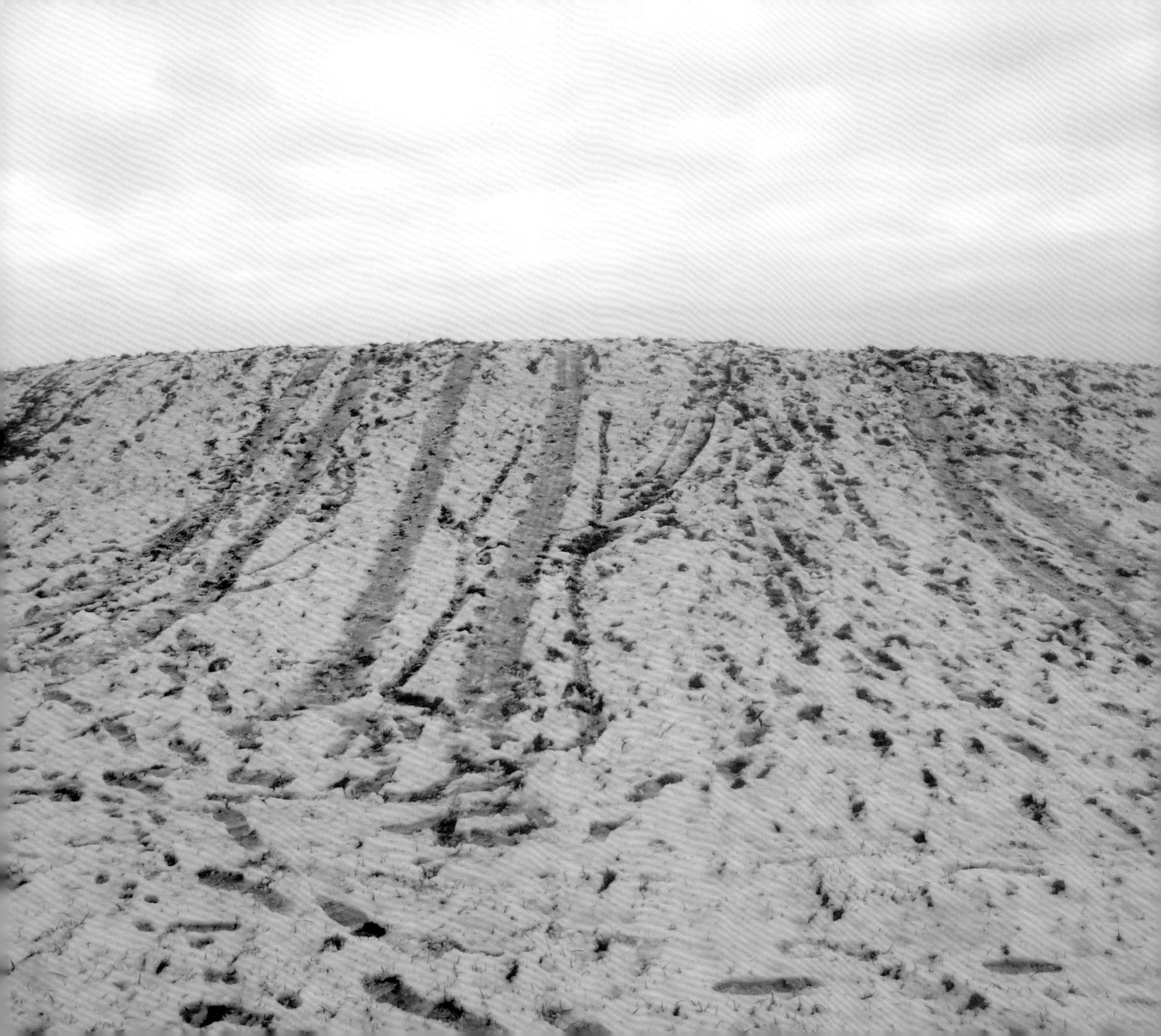

Opposite: Snow tracks, Hill of Tara, Co. Meath (January 2013)
Above: Love Heart shaped ice puddle, Hill of Tara, Co. Meath (January 2013)

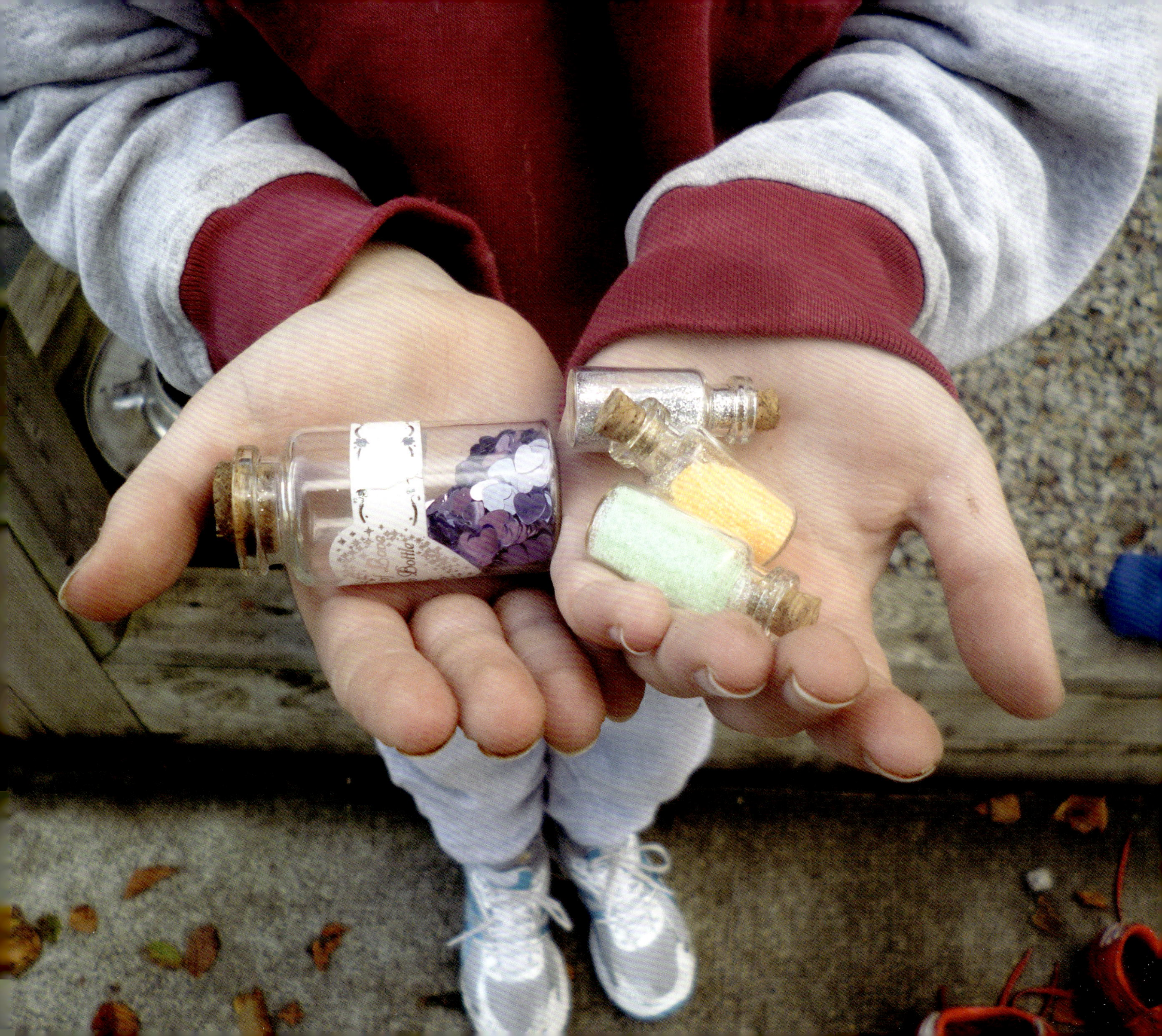

Good Luck

It is no surprise that Tara has a lot of superstition and belief related to it. While many sites associated with luck have slowly disappeared out of the minds and practices of many people, nearly every parish in the country had some place which when visited was believed to provide luck or cure a particular ailment.

Perhaps it is part human nature, part our culture, that we like to believe that by having certain things on our person, or by visiting certain places or doing certain things that we will be healed or get good luck.

One account of this nature is described in Steffi Finegan's story, a pupil from Skryne National School.

The story relayed to me was that some time ago, Steffi bought a jar of colourful fairy dust and small plastic love hearts in the gift shop on the hill. Every time she plays a match she places a love heart in her football stocking, which, she says, always brings good luck.

When I spoke with Mary Finegan, Steffi's mother, about getting a photo of the love hearts, Mary was surprised that she'd told me the story as she has an incredibly personal association with these love hearts. A close school friend of hers, Isabel, had tragically passed away that year and she bought the love hearts and fairy dust to sprinkle them on her little friend's grave. This was one of her ways of dealing with the loss of her friend and out of this action she has ascribed the remaining love hearts with a certain power, luck and hope.

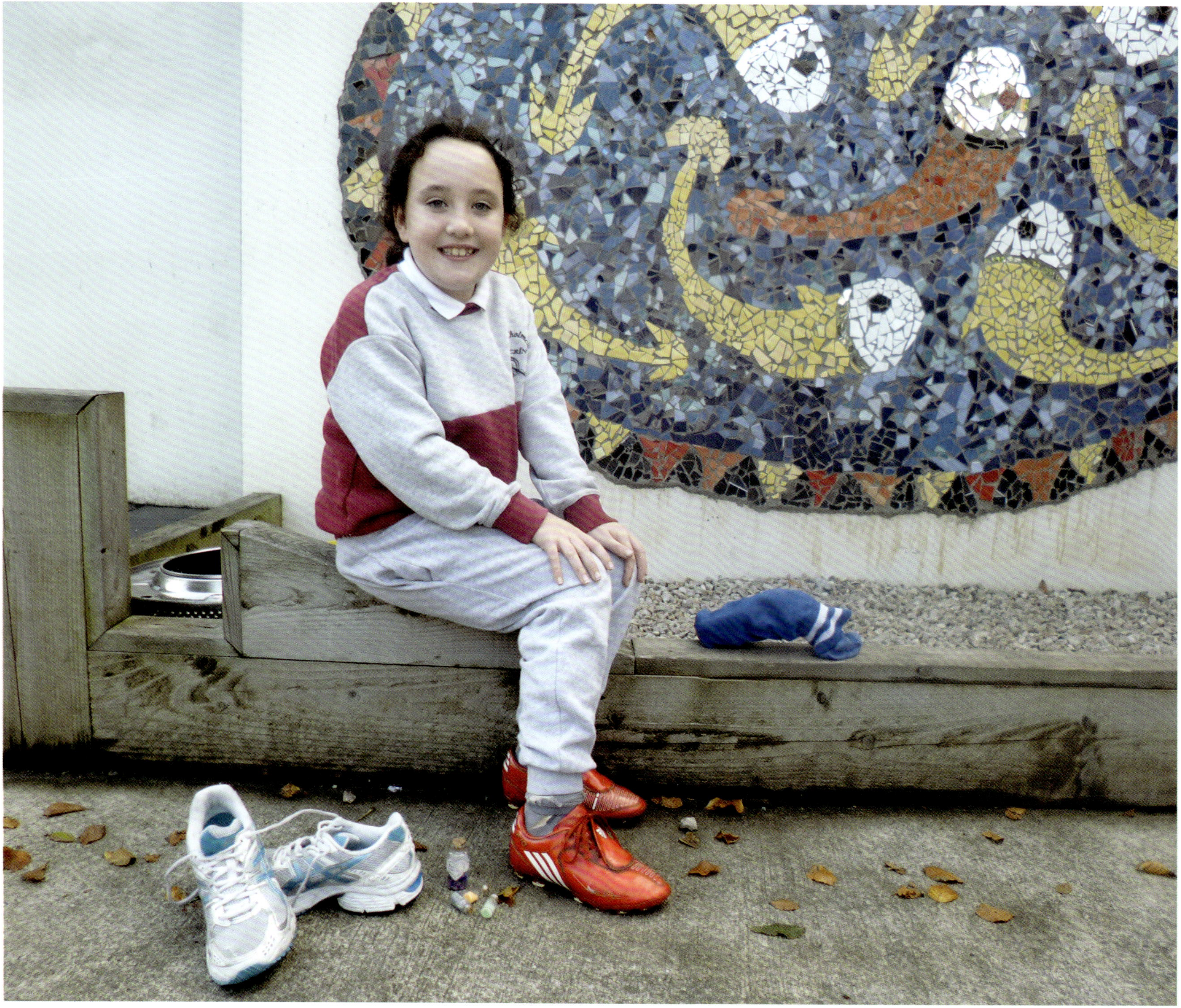

My story is about when I went to the hill of Tara and my nan bought a little tub of love hearts that said "would give you luck". When we got home, I put a love heart into my sock and went to play a important football match. We won and we have done really well ever since.

Opposite: Steffi Finegan, Skryne NS, Skryne, Co. Meath (October 2013)
Above: Account written by Sophie and Steffi Finegan, Skryne NS, Skryne, Co. Meath (January 2013)

My Stories About The Hill of Tara

The Fairy Tree

People love the fairy tree and I do too. ~~People make wishes with~~ People tie things to the tree and make wishes. Once when I went up to Tara, I took my bobbin out of my hair and tied it on the Fairy Tree. I wished for my very own pony and the next year I got a pony I was thrilled.

The Water from The Holy Well

My Nana loves walking on the Hill of Tara. One day she went the Holy Well and she took some water. When I sprained my fingers I went to her house and she blessed my fingers and she poured some Holy water.

Above: Emma McLoughlin and her pony
Opposite: Story written by Emma McLoughlin (February 2013)

Photo taken on family camera and scanned by Emma

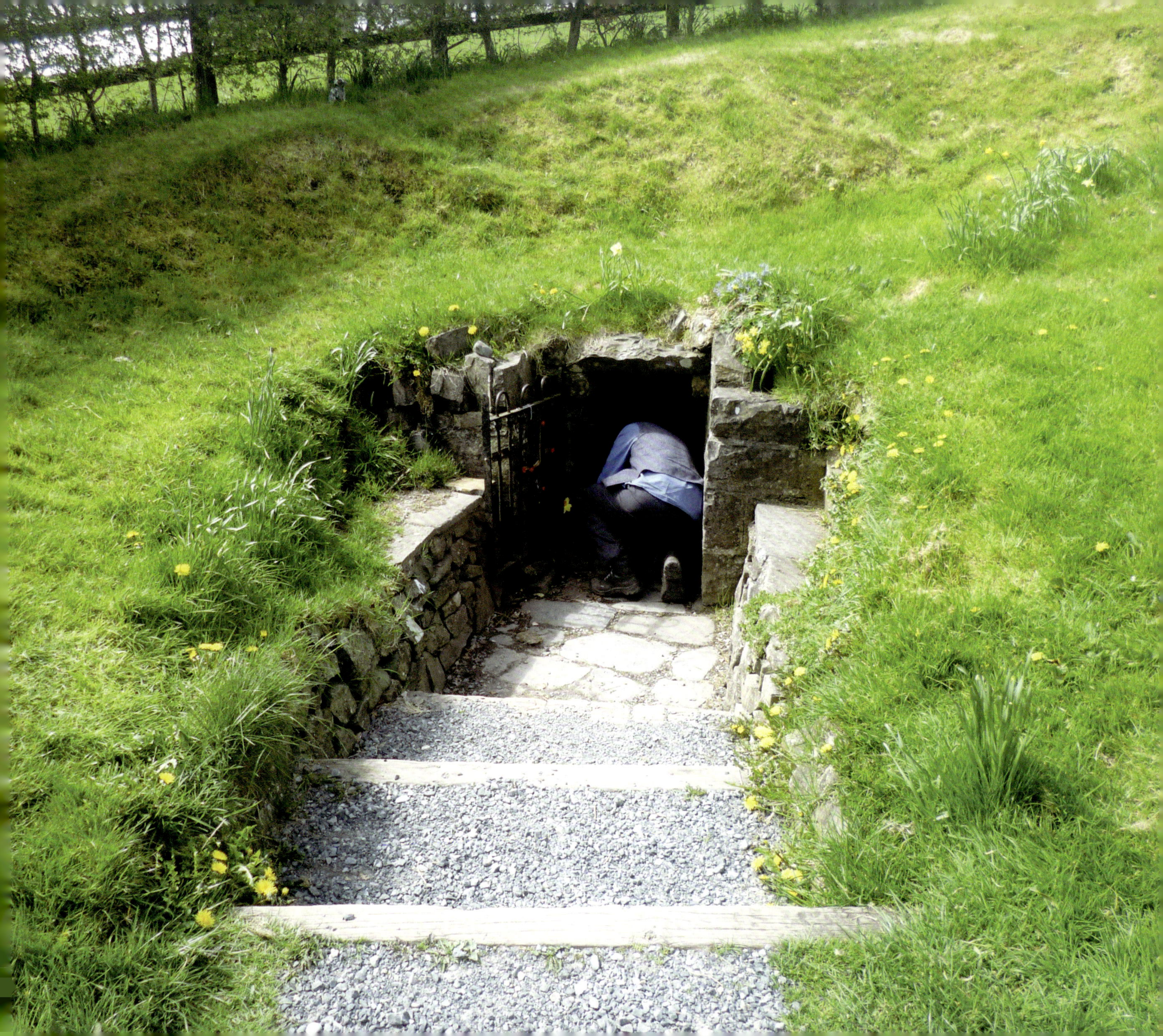

Small Country

It's often been said that there could never be a take on the TV programme/experiment *Big Brother* in Ireland, as if you put a group of 'Irish strangers' into a room, after a very short time talking, they'd be likely to realise that they were a friend of a friend, if not actually a distant relative. This happened when I stopped to talk to a lad in a Toyota Liteace van in the car park of Tara one morning in May. He was sitting in a back seat of the van, window open and eating porridge out of a saucepan that he'd just cooked it in. After a chat about who he was and who I was and what we were doing on the hill, he asked would I join him for a cup of tea. I said I would, so off we strolled, walking and talking, to the well for water. Back at the van he poured the water into the pot and placed it on his make-and-do stove. I told him water from a holy well wouldn't boil but he said he'd give it a go. As the water warmed up, we spoke about everything from traditional singers we knew, the holy wells on the hill and the rebels of 1798. Time was against me as I had to leave for Dublin so I said I wouldn't have time for the tea after all. Knowing I was from Wexford he asked could he sing me a parting song. As he sang *Kelly the Boy from Killanne* a popular Wexford '98 song, an older man with his dog strolled over to listen. When the song finished, he asked 'are ye from Wexford boys?'. I told him I was and the singer from 'the north'. As we spoke, the older man told me he was born in Wexford and moved to the Tara area when he was a child. He said he'd still know people there but couldn't remember the placenames. I bid the two good luck and said we'll meet again, while knowing well we probably wouldn't.

Four weeks later, I was dropping a tractor off in a neighbour's shed when the woman of the house came out and said 'I hear you were up on the Hill of Tara a few weeks ago'. She turned out to be the older man's relation and he'd phoned her when we parted. His name is Jasper Bennett and he walks the hill every day. His dog's name was Buffy, and by chance, this neighbour's dog answers to the same name. I think the man in the van was called Aengus. I never found out where he was from - 'from the north' was the most I got. He said he would make it to Wexford for the strawberries and the new spuds in June.

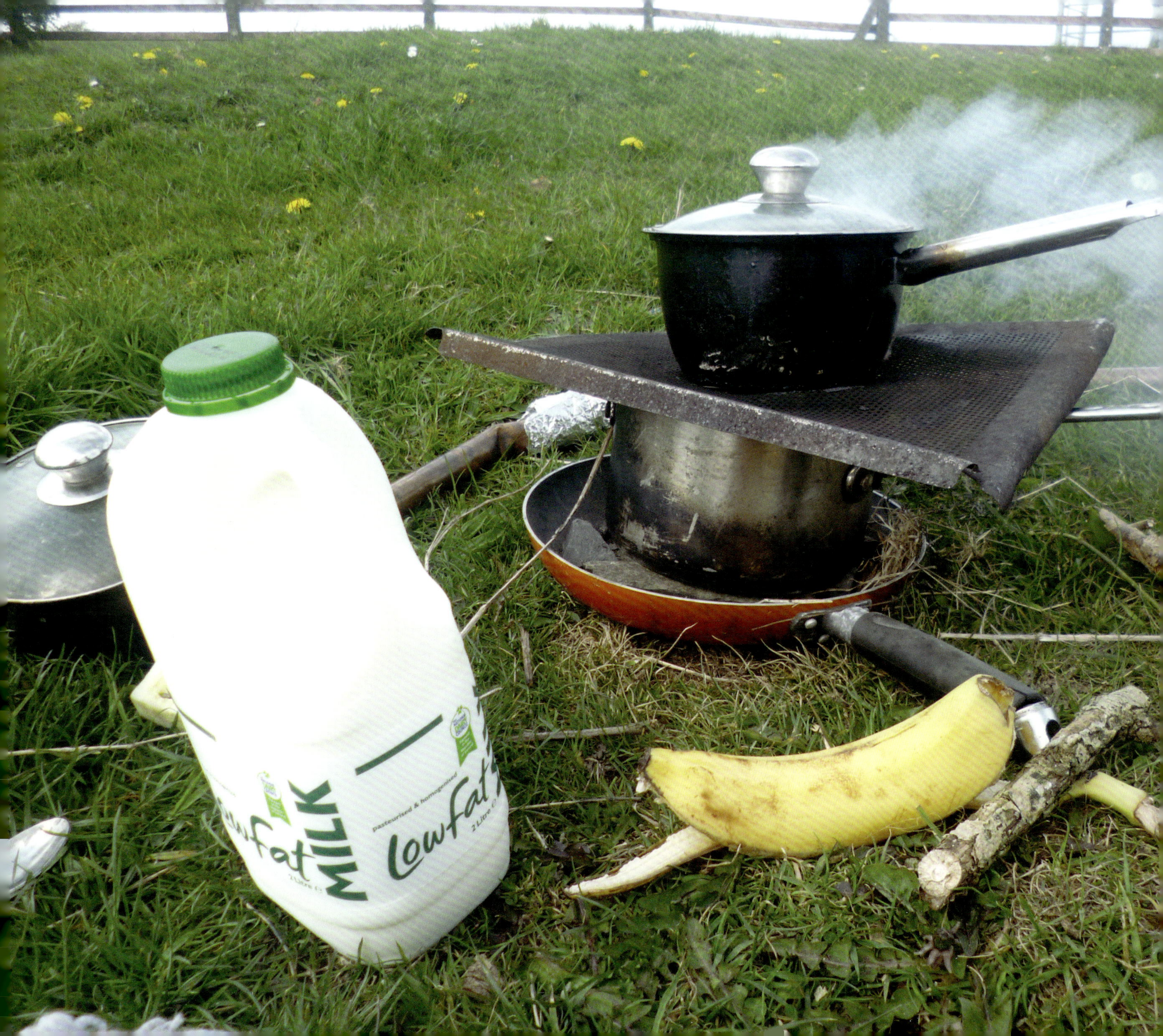
lowfat MILK
pasteurised & homogenised
lowfat

Opposite: Aengus boiling water for tea, Hill of Tara, Co. Meath (May 2013)
Above: Aengus singing, Hill of Tara, Co. Meath (May 2013)

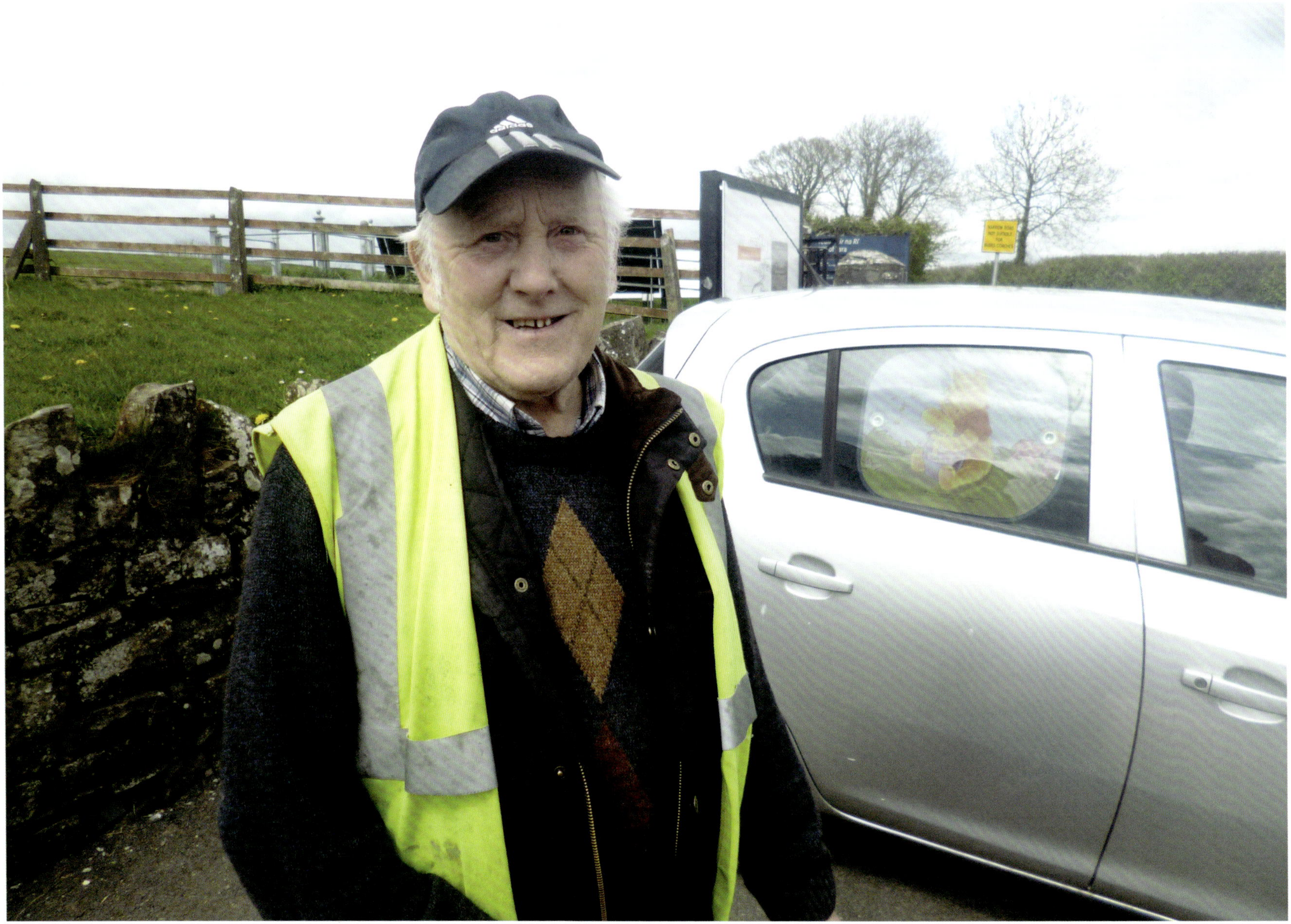

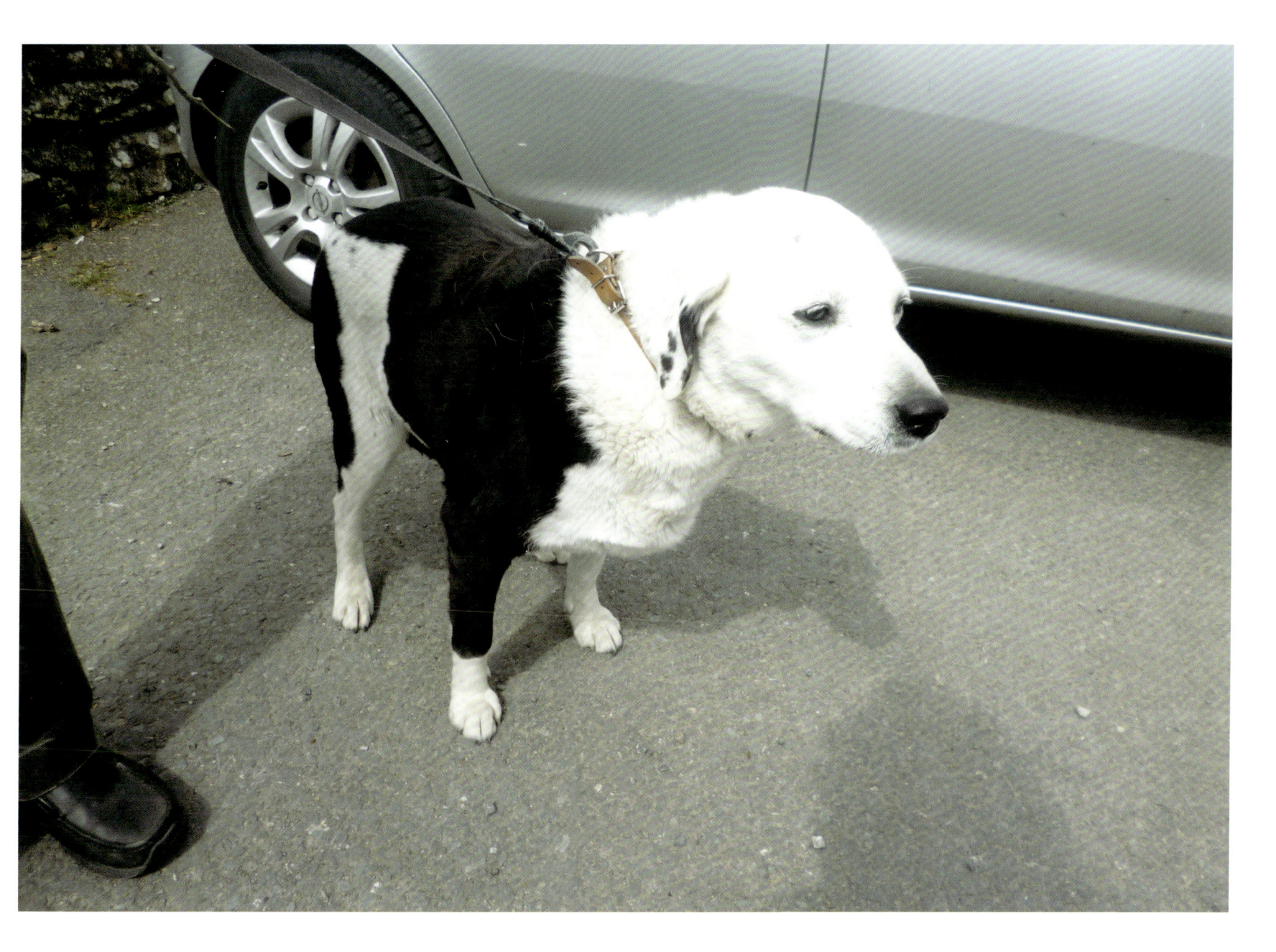

Opposite: Jasper Bennett, Hill of Tara, Co. Meath (May 2013)
Above: Buffy, Hill of Tara, Co. Meath (May 2013)

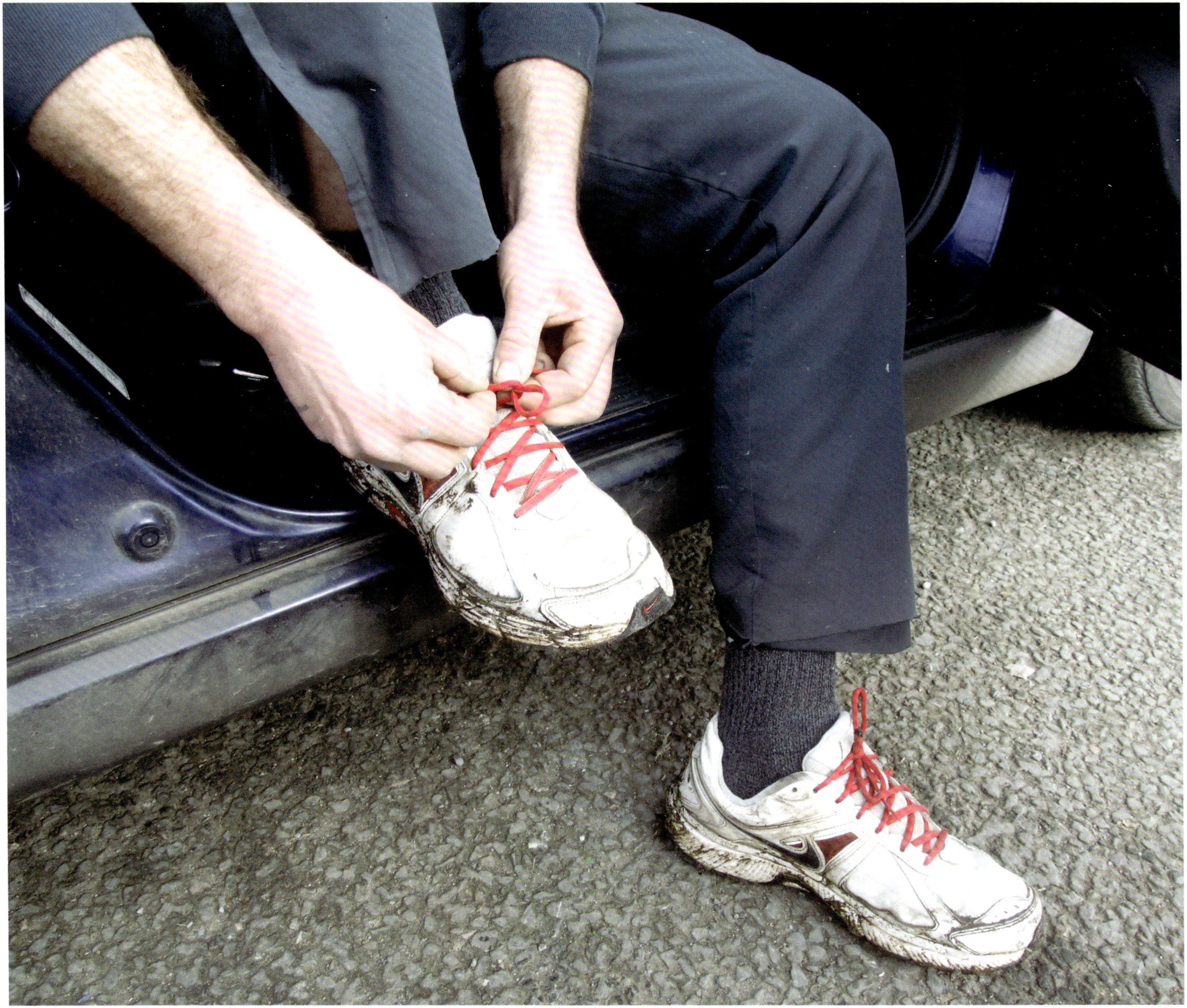

The Energy Fields

In recent memory ex Meath Football manager Sean Boylan made the hill popular as a place for physical and psychological training of his team. In fact, I was informed by the daughter of the present manager, Mick O'Dowd, that the team still trains on the hill. She attends Skryne NS and explained that she accompanies the team when they train and that her father 'goes up there for luck so they might win'.

The hill has a natural attraction for those interested in outdoor pursuits from physical endurance workouts to a genteel stroll, cross-country running or simply walking the dog. Tara attracts hundreds of people every day of the week. Like a park in a city or town, it draws people from far and near. It provides a perfect package for the stroller: space, history, fresh air and coffee. And now in a time where walking and outdoor pursuits are experiencing a height in popularity, Tara is the envy of any county in regard to that matter.

The Annual Tara Dawn Run is embraced by the whole county and beyond. This annual event is held in or around the summer Solstice and attracts hundreds of participants, young and old and at all levels of fitness. The 4km run begins in the dark of night at 4am. By the time the first runners cross the finish line the sun has begun to rise, illuminating them and the landscape before them.

In contrast to this group public event, cyclist Ricky Geoghegan cycles on the hill regularly throughout the year. Ricky, an ultra-distance cyclist from Trim, emailed me a few months prior to our first meeting. He cycled up the hill to meet me on a scorching hot day. He said the cycle wasn't much, just a half an hour.

We chatted in the car park about things in general, hopping from one thing to another, me resting against the bonnet of my car and him leaning on his bike. We spoke about keeping the mind going and having things to do. As an 'ultra-cyclist' the sheer tasks he undertakes are incredible, almost incomprehensible, yet he speaks about it so casually. He told me that a few years back he cycled non-stop from Malin Head to Mizen Head, and then back to Malin Head in a time of 55 hours and 37 minutes. I get tired walking from the carpark to the Lia Fáil. What does that say? Exactly.

Tara

My favourit thing about the hill of tara is the cross-country training. I love to run up and down the hills and at the end of the year we go into the coffee shop an get hot chocolate. But my favourite thing is to run down to the swings. My least favourit thing to do is run in the summer when all the flowers have bloomed and when we have to run through them or run when its very hot.

Tara

I love going to the hill of Tara because I go training with my dad. He is the Meath manager. He told me he goes up there for luck so they might win a game. I also love the well. People say that when that when you drop a coin in and make a wish, it comes true. The well has big rocks on the side. There is a beanch beside it and the water is very deep. In the summer the coins sparkle in the water. That whey i love Tara!

Opposite: Account written by Ellie Murphy, Skryne NS, Skryne, Co. Meath (March 2013)
Above: Account written by Amy O'Dowd, Skryne NS, Skryne, Co. Meath (March 2013)

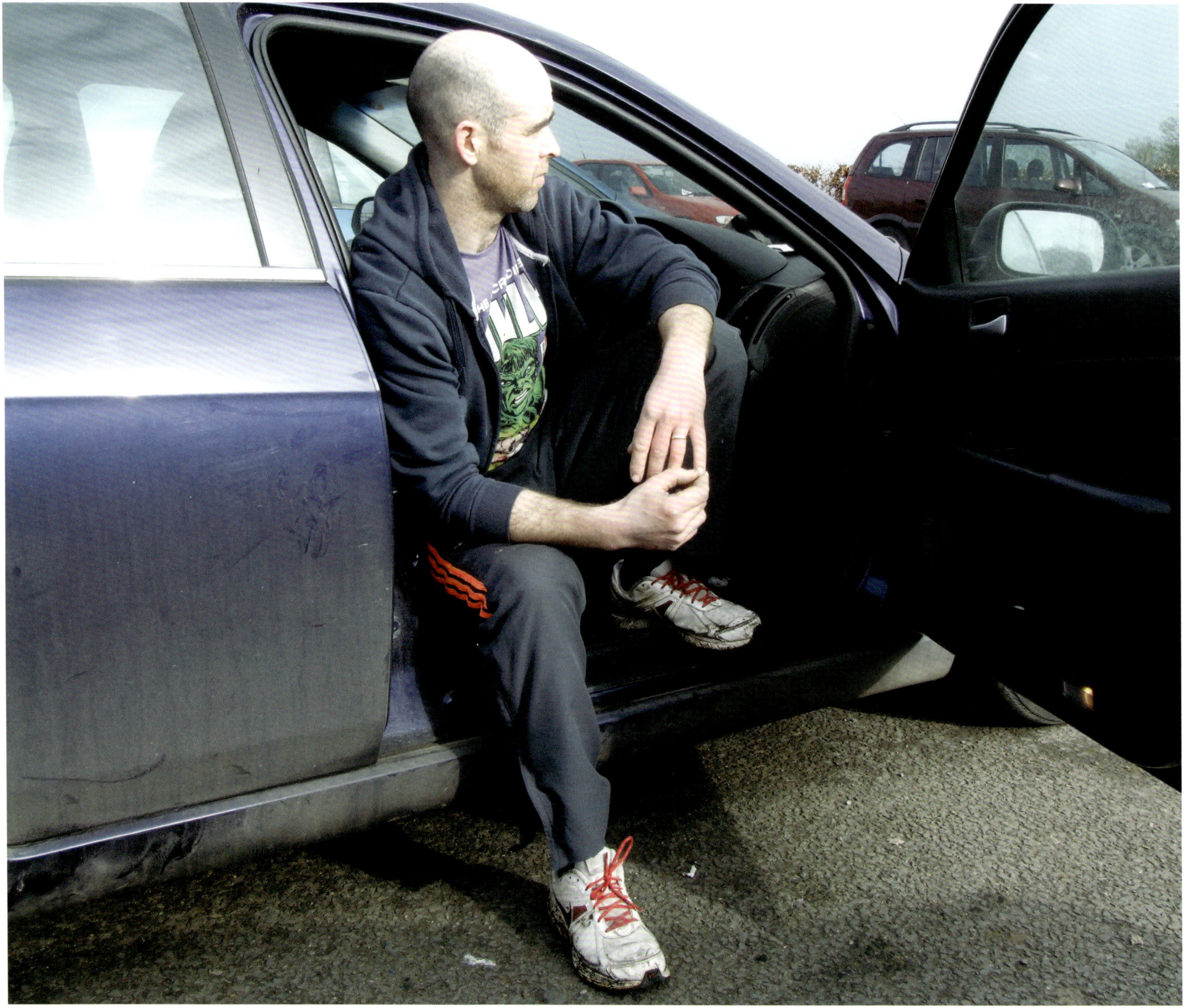

Opposite: Alan Kearney, Hill of Tara, Co. Meath (February 2013)
Above: Ricky Geoghegan, Hill of Tara, Co. Meath (June 2013)

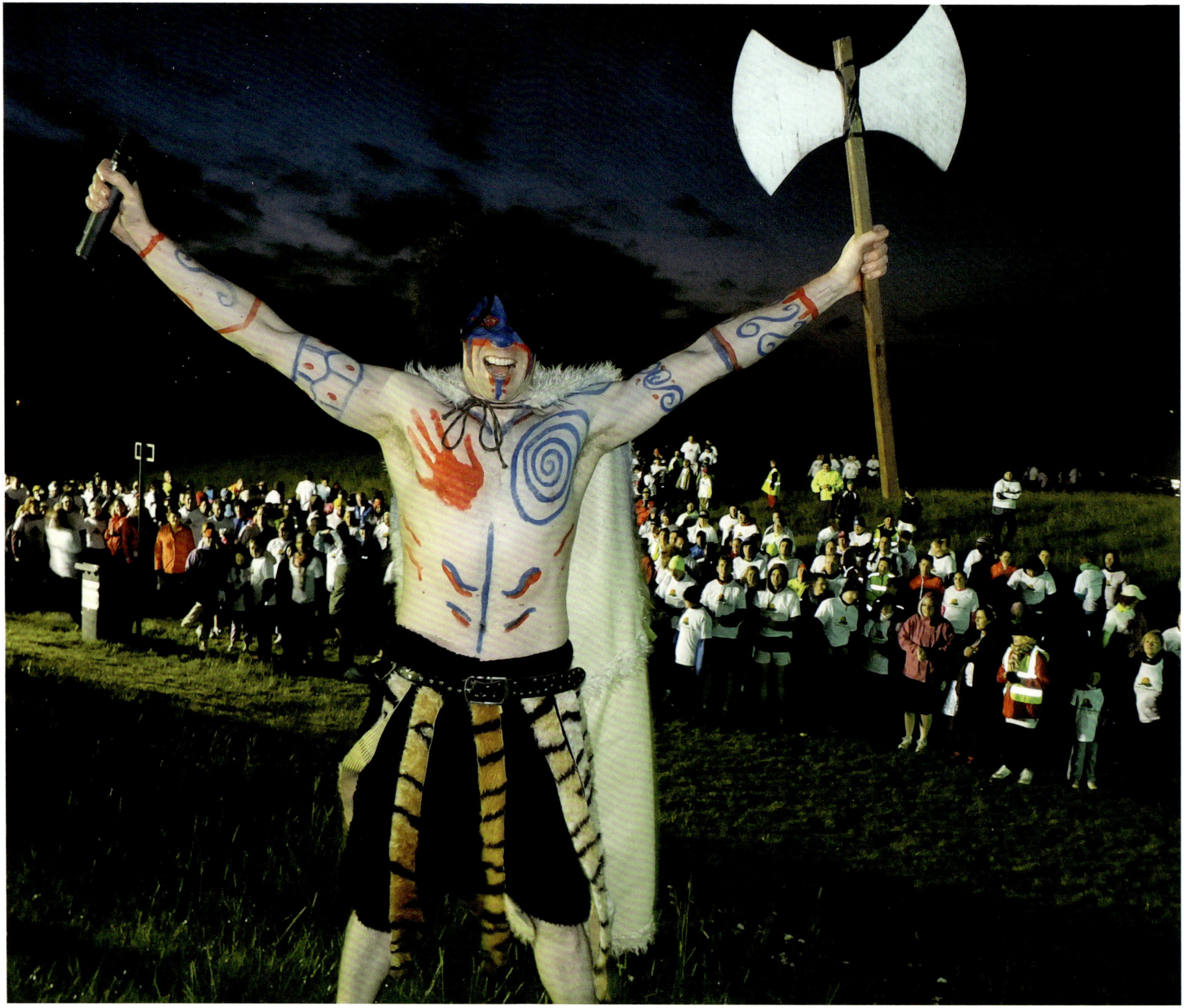

Above: Racing the Rising Sun at the Tara Dawn Run, Hill of Tara, Co. Meath (June 2013) Photo by Tom Bannon
Opposite: The Wildman of Tara, Tara Dawn Run, Hill of Tara, Co. Meath (June 2013) Photo by Tom Bannon

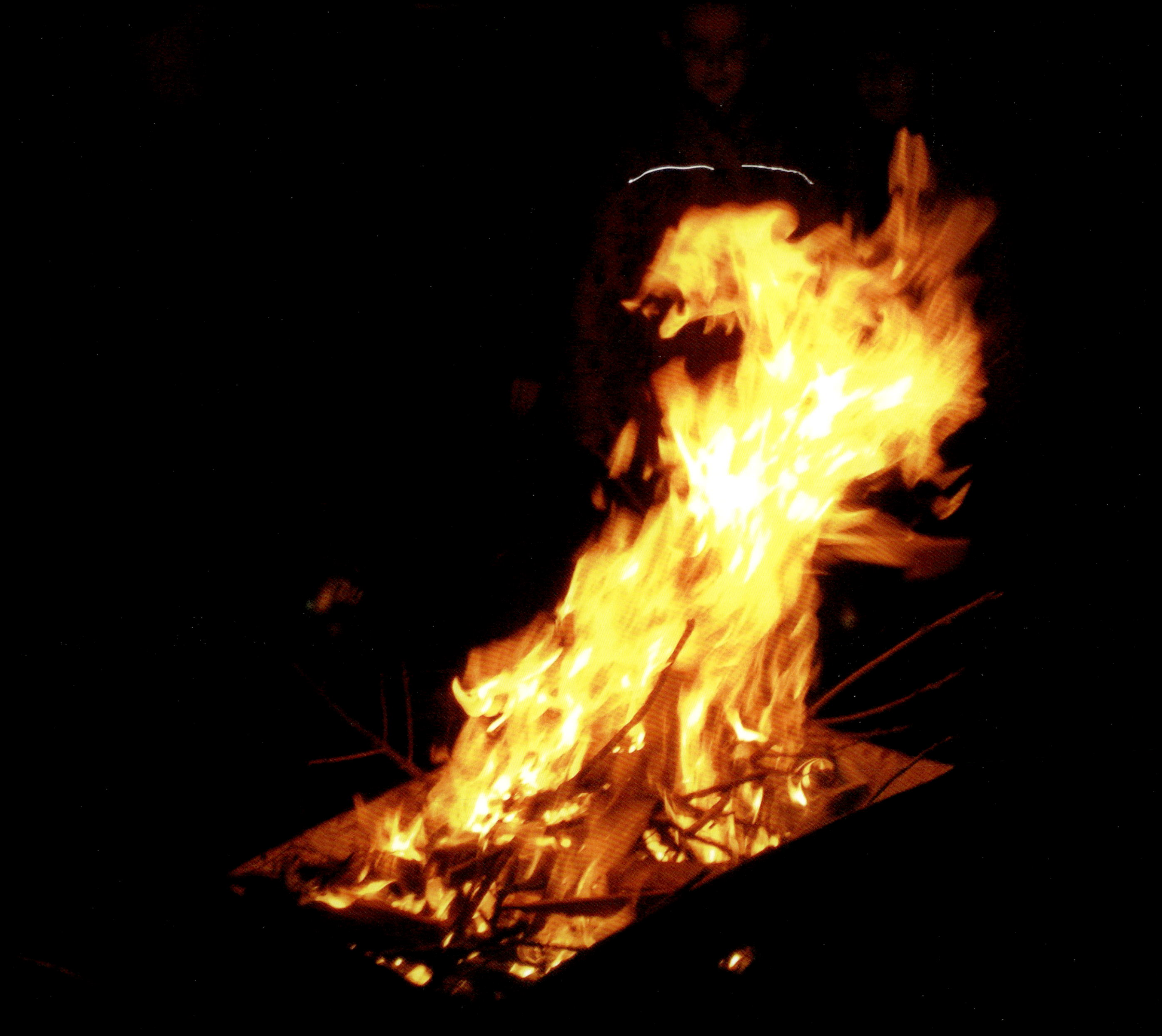

Fire

Fire is a strong symbol, and a physical elemental event in itself. Bonfires are associated with calendar rituals, celebrations and events. To this day we find Hallowe'en bonfires in inner-city Dublin, St. John's Eve fires in Mayo or Cork City or roadside bonfires to celebrate football matches or weddings.

Fire and the Hill of Tara go hand in hand. Pagan and Christian, ancient and contemporary, the symbol of fire has always had a connection to the hill. Today the tradition continues with the Navan Shamrock Festival where the fire is lit on the hill and relayed to Navan by torch by a local biker troupe. In a true turn of genius or 'guntering', an old metal wheelbarrow hosts the fire on the Hill of Tara. The wheelbarrow protects the ground from fire damage, as well as being an easy device to move and empty when done.

Caragh Conway from Skryne National School brought me the photo (opposite) she took on the 13th of March 2013; we can just about see the outline of the people gathered around the fire in the wheelbarrow.

Another story that grabbed me was from Bláithin Moran who emailed me to tell me why the hill is important to her. After a few general emails at the start Bláithin told me that she had been involved in an accident just months beforehand in September 2012 and that her boyfriend Fionán passed away as a result. She was badly injured but thankfully recovered. In October, Bláithin and about fifty close family and friends came together and had a farewell party for Fionán on the hill. Music, chat and fire were the main ingredients of the night as they recounted stories relating to him. The three photos opposite were taken on the night on a camera phone.

Tara Project - Getting Back Finally :)

blaithin moran
To: Michael Fortune <mytaraproject@gmail.com>

Tue, Apr 9, 2013 at 10:03 PM

Hello Michael!

Oh it was crazy with all the relatives. Ok cool, I'll attach the picture with this email and if you need a better quality one I shall try get you one.
The story behind it is this. My boyfriend Fionán and I were in a automobile accident back in the September 2012. Fionán passed away, I was badly injured but thankfully I made it, and I am still recovering but doing well. Tara Hill was always a special place for not only Fionán and I , but also all of our friends. We used to and still do go out for walks and just talk about what times must have been like back in the time of the high kings and wondering what "the land we are lying on" had seen etc. Daydreaming really, but there is always a positive spiritual vibe on the site of Tara Hill, as there is at Loughcrew, where we also visit frequently.

At the end of October we asked for permission to have a gathering at one of the areas just adjacent to the site, we were given permission and there were guitars, songs and a little fire and lanterns let go and fireworks went off. There were roughly fifty friends and family present and it was a great night with a lot of spirituality and love. All being doing with utmost respect of where we were. We all had a real connection to Fionán there and we knew he was there with us. This is basically the gist of our story :)

[Quoted text hidden]

--
Bláithín Moran

tara1.jpg
68K

Opposite: Email sent from Bláithín Moran (April 2013)
Above: Photos taken on mobile phone, Hill of Tara, Co. Meath (October 2012)

Light and Dark

I met Irenijus Lebedis on the eve of the Solstice stationed in his car at the road entrance to what is commonly known as the Banqueting Hall. He was providing security for the OPW over the night of the Solstice gathering on the 21st of June 2013. Originally from Lithuania, he now works between Ireland and Germany.

Irenijus told me that on the day of the summer Solstice in his home country of Lithuania, people go into the forest in search of a small flower found growing on ferns. The flower, known as 'Paparcio Ziedas', brings good luck to those who find it. He recalled collecting the flower when he was younger. We chatted for a good while more and then parted company for the night.

A short while later I spoke with some of the people gathered for the Solstice. When I mentioned the security on site, they referred to them as 'mercenaries keeping the people away from their sacred site'. Next morning I woke to witness the Solstice sunrise, and was greeted by many of the same revellers, holding hands and chanting to the sound of a Tibetan bowl and the scent of burning sage. As I slipped away from witnessing this performance, I wondered whether in fact the 'mercenary' was more in tune with his own folk belief than the group holding hands in a circle on the hill…

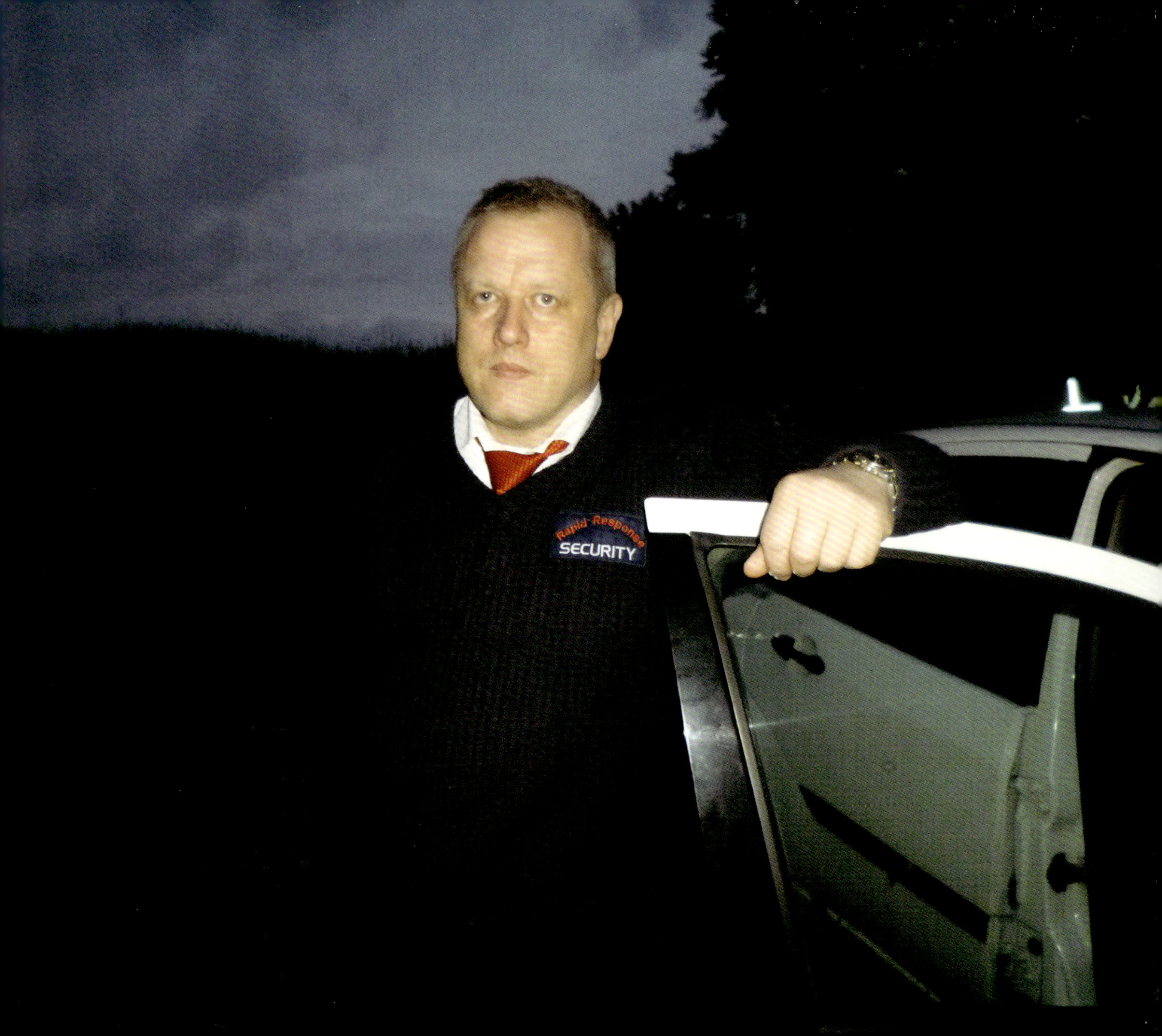
Rapid Response
SECURITY

Opposite: Irenijus Lebedis, Hill of Tara, Co. Meath (June 2013)
Above: Irenijus Lebedis holds a flower, Hill of Tara, Co. Meath (June 2013)

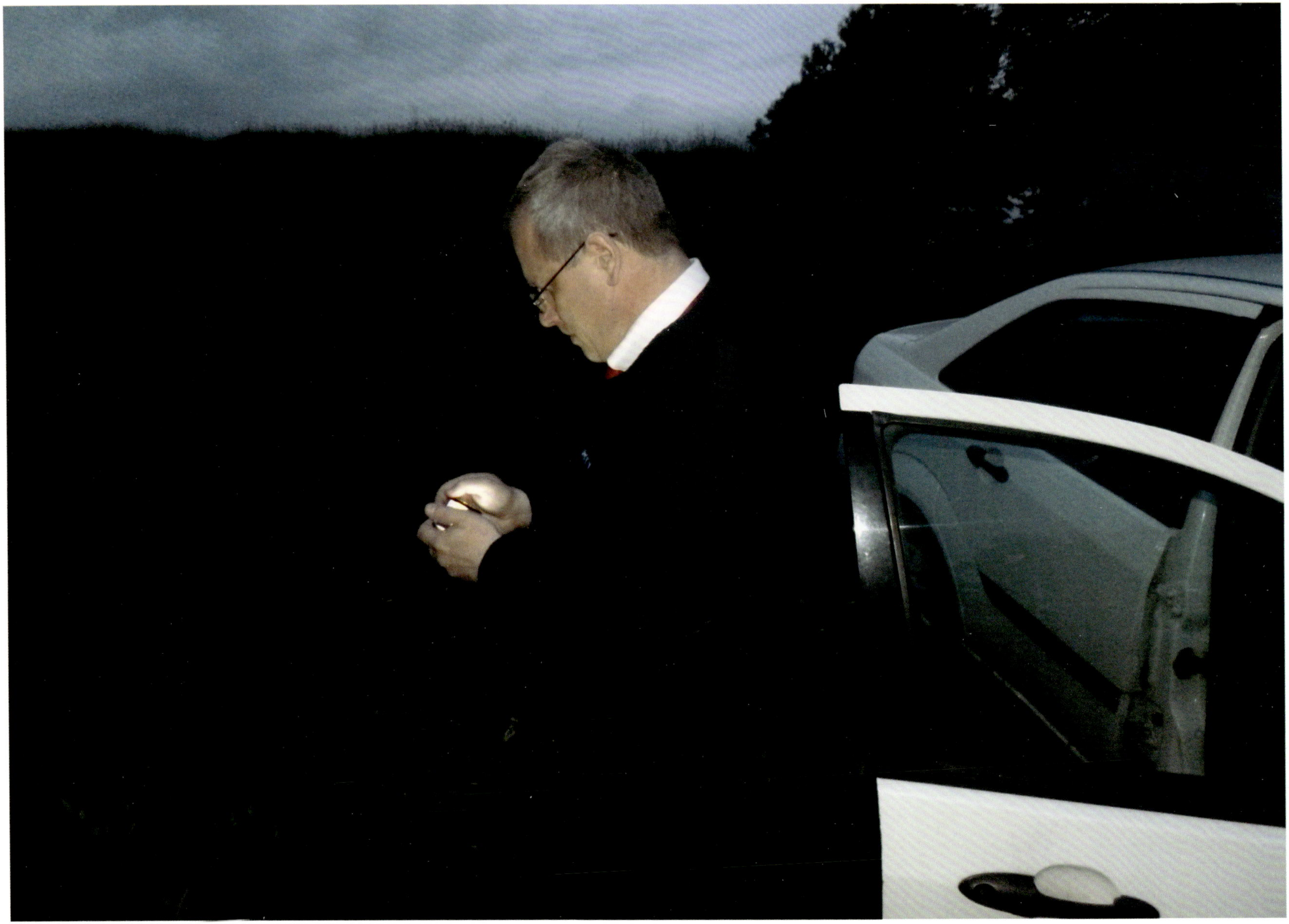

Opposite: Kyrie Murray shows me orbs in photographs he took, Hill of Tara, Co. Meath (June 2013)
Above: Irenijus Lebedis seaching for image of flower to show me on phone, Hill of Tara, Co. Meath (June 2013)

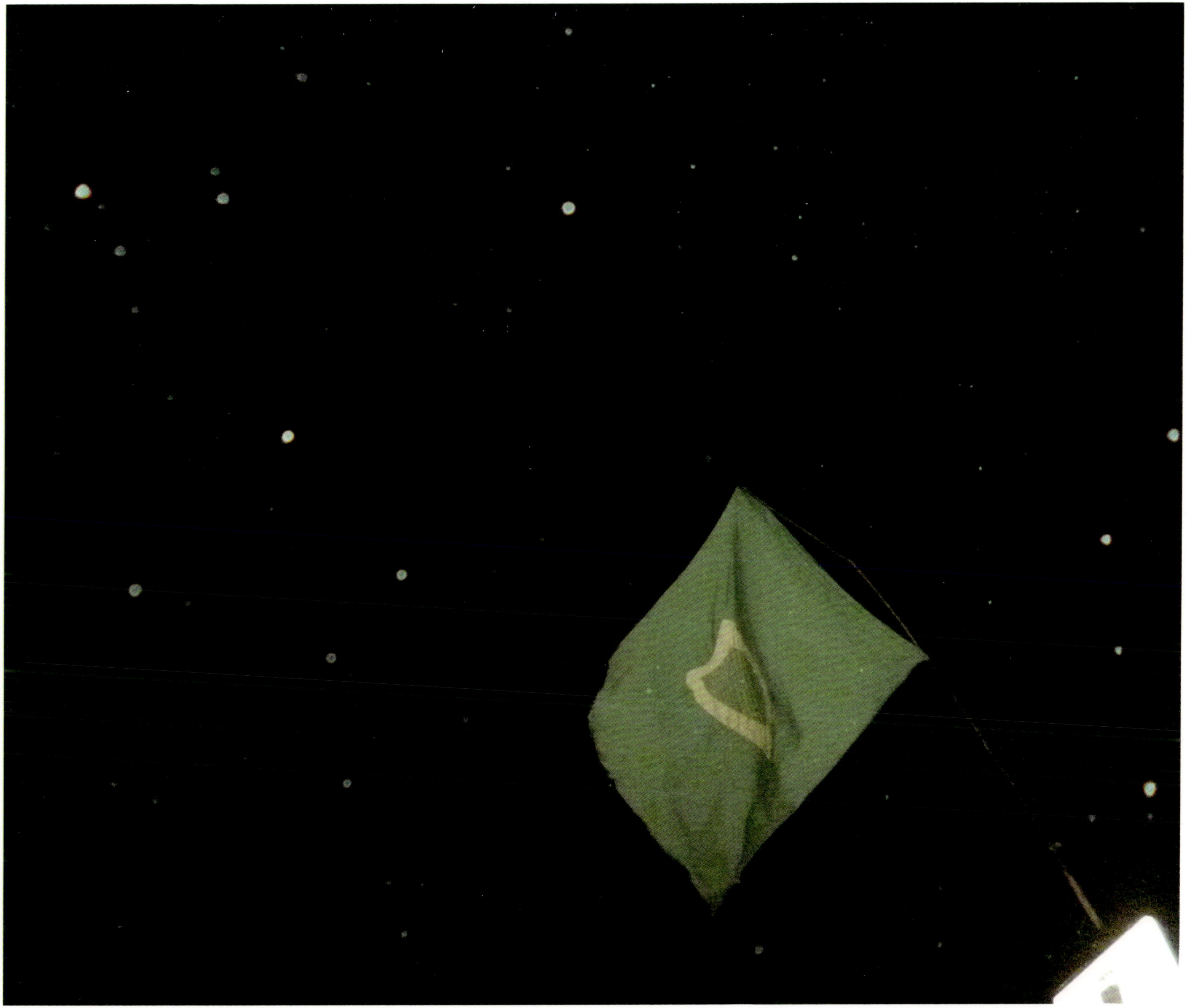

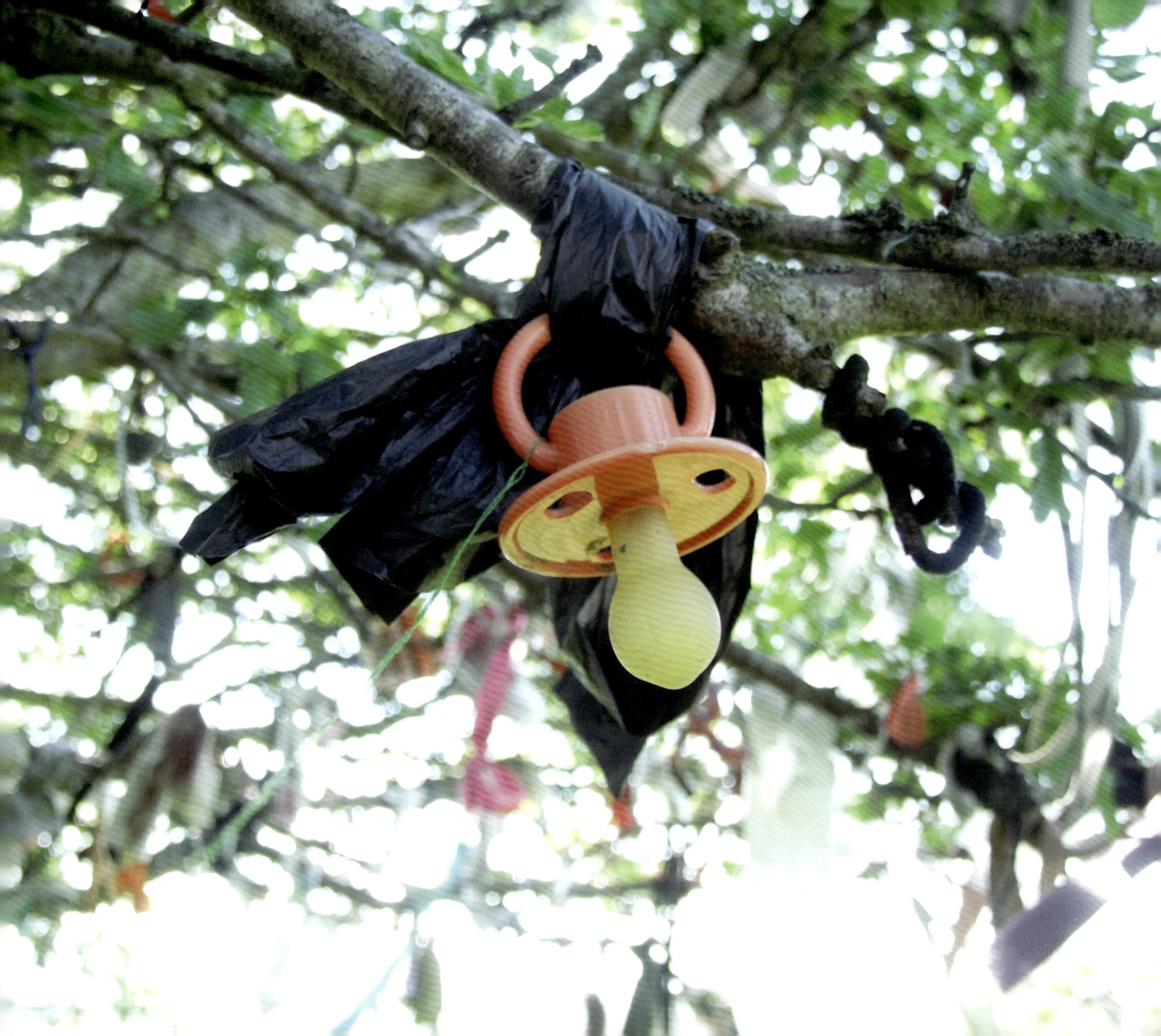

Biography

Michael Fortune grew up in a family immersed in story, superstition and folk belief in an area known as 'The Macamores', an old Gaelic stronghold stretching along the east coast of County Wexford. He completed his BA in Fine Art, specialising in video and performance at Limerick School of Art and Design and his MA in Film at Dún Laoghaire School of Film.

Working predominantly in film and photography, much of his practice revolves around the collection of material - material which he generates out of the relationships and experiences he develops with the people he encounters. The intimate nature of the relationships with the people and circumstances he encounters, and the subsequent reflective treatment of the material at hand, is a key feature of his work.

Much of Fortune's work borrows from the popular conventions of film, home video, snap photography and the printed media and his work can be seen as growing out of a tradition of social documentary and anthropological film. He combines the stand-alone idiosyncrasies of people and incidents in everyday life, with complex and visually careful and contemplative treatments that adeptly handle the aesthetics of repetition, humour, obscurity, strangeness and intimacy. He has been the recipient of numerous awards and bursaries for his work, which he presents extensively nationally and internationally in a variety of contexts, ranging from gallery exhibitions through to single screen presentations in film and video art festivals.

Due to the ethnographic nature of his practice he has been commissioned to undertake various folklore collections and traditional song research and performance projects throughout Ireland. These have been presented in a variety of spaces ranging from libraries and contemporary art spaces to village halls and handball alleys. He is a regular visitor to the Folklore Department in University College Cork and his collections are housed in numerous universities and libraries in North America and Europe.

His ability to explore and celebrate the nuances of identity, place, ritual and story have been well demonstrated and are central to the success of his project work. He has championed the use of new media such as film, photography and web design since the late 1990's and has produced a vast collection of material and content which has been presented in a variety of forms.

Since 2008 he has been working with the National Library of Ireland on a series of traditional song research and performance projects in conjunction with Age and Opportunity, the Irish Traditional Music Archive and the Arts Council. In late 2013 he produced a new project for the library, entitled 'Man, Woman and Child', a traditional song project based on the Child Ballad Collection, which was supported by the above partners. He is currently developing a new strand of this project for the library, with the support of the Arts Council and The World Music Academy in Limerick, which will be launched in late 2014. Other 2014 projects include, 'MEET – The Mobile Pub', which was commissioned as part of the Limerick City of Culture and 'About This Place' which was commissioned by Wexford County Council.

Michael currently works as a part-time Assistant Lecturer in Limerick School of Art and continues to conduct long and short-term project work in communities and institutions the length and breadth of Ireland. He continues to live and work in rural Wexford, having moved inland to another old Gaelic stronghold, 'The Duffry', which lies at the foot of Mount Leinster in north west Wexford. Here he lives with his partner, Aileen Lambert and their young children.

Further information on Michael and his projects can be found at www.folklore.ie, www.asirovedout.ie, www.aboutthisplace.ie, www.homespun.ie and www.manwomanandchild.ie

Opposite: The Dodie Tree, Hill of Tara, Co. Meath (April 2013)

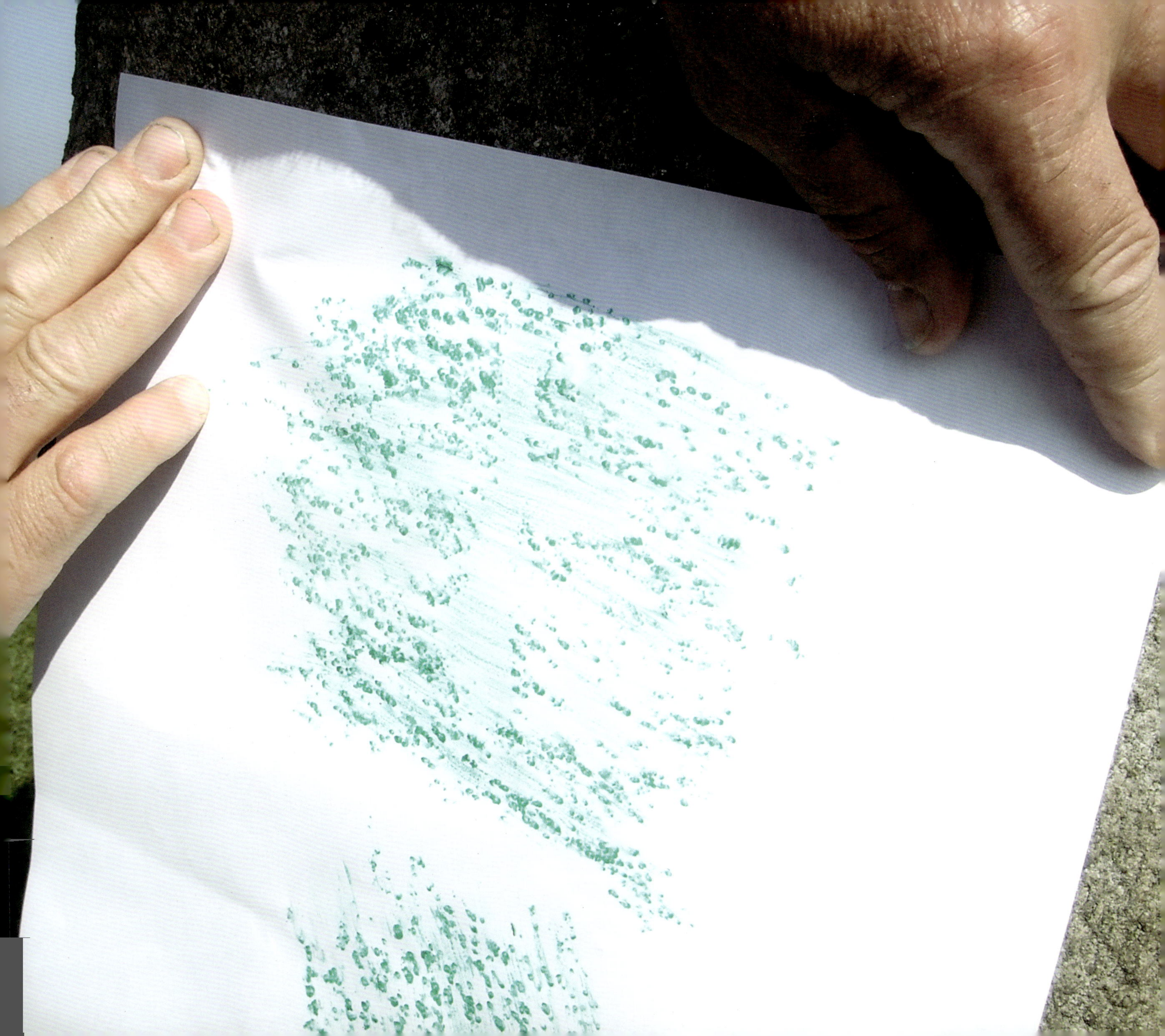

Acknowledgements

Thanks to Loreto Guinan, Gerardette Bailey and Cathy Martin, from the Heritage and Arts Offices of Meath County Council for their vision and support throughout this process.

Thanks to all in Scoil Cholmcille National School, Skryne for all their help and assistance - staff and pupils. The open-door and welcome was always there with whatever I needed throughout. So thank you Martin Kennedy (Principal), Andrew Whelan (6th), Grainne Harrington (4th/5th) and Kieran Fanning (3rd/4th). Without your help Kieran, I wouldn't have got this far. Thanks to all the pupils who contributed stories. Although I only used some in the book, the rest of your stories and accounts helped me along the way. Thanks also to the parents of many of these pupils whom I bothered with questions and photo requests. Thanks to the Rooney family for allowing me to use the story connected with their daughter, Isabel, in the book.

Other people to thank are Ger Clarke, Maurice and Mary Cassidy, Jasper Bennett, Michael Slavin, Alan Kearney, Anne-Marie Durkan, Richard Farrelly, Martha McCabe, Dan McCabe, Brian Oliver, Bláithin Moran, Jimmy Rafter, Sean Marmion, John Jameson, Shane Holland, Breda Marron, Fionnuala Gryson, Fred Simmons, Kevin McCaffrey, Patrick Daly, Terence Doran, Adam Fulton, Ricky Geoghegan, Keith Rowe, Pedro Almeida, Jill Jacob and family, Louise Hayes, John Donohoe (*Meath Chronicle*), Paddy Pryle, Sinéad Burke (Navan Traveller Training Centre), Irenijus Lebedis, Michael McGuire, Hugh Mc Nelis, Carmel Diviney, Mary Wilkinson, Schira Conway, Teresa Powderly, Mary Finegan, Aileen Lambert, Jerry Doyle, Joan Lambert, Mary O'Regan, Amy O'Regan, Margaret Allen, Kyrie Murray, Willie Foley and Mick Dempsey from the OPW in Trim, James and all involved in the Tara Dawn Run, Lillie Byrne and photographer Tom Bannon for the use of his photographs in this book.

Commissioned and published by Meath County Council.
Edited and compiled by Michael Fortune.
Design: Two Heads Design & Advertising.
Printing: WG Baird.

All images copyright Michael Fortune unless otherwise stated.
End Image: Lillie Byrne. All rights reserved.
ISBN 978 1 900923 28 6

Opposite: Ger Clarke holds rubbing of cross carving on Lia Fáil (June 2013)

ISBN 978-1-900923-28-6